"*Essential Habits of Relational Leaders* is all about intentional investment in others—richer relationships and more effective leadership are dividends from building relational equity. Becoming a relational leader not only enlarges our leadership capacity, it is also the key to effective discipleship. In this book, Boyd Bailey provides practical principles to cultivate deeper, more meaningful relationships with spouses, family, friends and coworkers. The points to ponder and takeaways in each chapter guide the reader through reflection and self-evaluation to habit-building application and action. Boyd helped me to identify and shore up relational deficits and to begin compounding eternal investments."

David Martin, VP, Strategy & Business Development

"With this book, Boyd Bailey models the dignity of simplicity by supplying actionable key takeaways. He clearly articulates the compound interest relational leaders gain by taking an inside-out approach."

Jason Davis, Stewardship Coach, Jericho Force Enterprises

"What better person is there to write a book on relational leadership than Boyd Bailey? Boyd is a personal family friend and is known in our community for his ever-intentional investments in people. He states, 'Our life purpose is fulfilled when we can help another fulfill their life purpose.' Profound. In *Essential Habits of Relational Leaders*, Boyd is ever so artfully instructing us on a recipe that has been passed down since the time of Christ: Love God and Love People. Love others and seek their best interest without expecting anything in return. What kind of profound impact would this have if humans did this naturally? I highly recommend reading this book to get better in tune with your own heart, and by doing so, inevitably you will be able to better love those around you.

Zack Bowe, husband, father, and
Cataract Refractive Account Manager, Alcon Labs

ESSENTIAL HABITS

OF

RELATIONAL LEADERS

BOYD BAILEY

HARVEST HOUSE PUBLISHERS
EUGENE, OREGON

Cover design by Bryce Williamson

Cover photo © Dmitirii_Guzhanin / Gettyimage

For bulk, special sales, or ministry purchases, please call 1-800-547-8979. Email: Customerservice@hhpbooks.com

Essential Habits of Relational Leaders
Copyright © 2020 by Boyd Bailey
Published by Harvest House Publishers
Eugene, Oregon 97408
www.harvesthousepublishers.com

ISBN 978-0-7369-7556-8 (pbk)
ISBN 978-0-7369-7799-9 (eBook)

Library of Congress Cataloging-in-Publication Data is on file at the Library of Congress, Washington, DC.

Printed in the United States of America

20 21 22 23 24 25 26 27 28 / BP-RD / 10 9 8 7 6 5 4 3 2 1

To my four sons-in-law: Todd, Tripp, J.T., and Tyler,
who model well being relational leaders
at home, at work, and in life.

Acknowledgments

Thank you Wisdom Hunters team for loving like Jesus: Rita Bailey, Shanna Schutte, Rachel Snead, Rachel Prince, Tripp Prince, Susan Fox, Patti Brown, and Wendy Becker.

Thank you, National Christian Foundation, for the opportunity to reach and restore every person through the love of Christ and to mobilize resources by inspiring biblical generosity.

I am grateful to our community group for keeping it real! Life is twice as blessed and half as hard because of you: Betsy and Bill Chapman, Alison and Bill Ibsen, Aria and Josh Randolph, Jodi and Andy Ward, and best of all, my sweetheart Rita Isbill Bailey.

Finishing Well accountability guys, thanks for deep "scuba diving" conversations, instead of shallow "snorkeling" small talk: Frank Bell, Woody Faulk, Mike Kendrick, and Scotland Wright.

To all the book clubs, you are the best: members of the Businessmen Book Club—David Deeter, Nathan Deeter, and Mike Davis; members of Classics Book Club—Larry Green, Bill Ibsen, and Bill Williams; and members of the NCF Book Club—Greg Winchester, Greg Mauldin, and Michael King.

I am grateful to our family for supporting me: Rita, Rebekah, Todd, Hudson, Harrison, Marshall, Rachel, Tripp, Lily, Emmie, Charlie, Bethany, J.T., Weston, M.J., Anna, Tyler, and Wilson.

Thank you, Susan Fox, for your expert editing. Thanks go to Terry Glaspey for coaching me, brainstorming with me, and bringing out the best in me and my writing. You know me better than I know me!

Thank you, Wisdom Hunters Board of Directors, for your love, prayers, and accountability—Cliff Bartow, Andrew Wexler, and John Hightower, and to the advisors, Debbie Ochs and Jack McEntee.

Thank you, Harvest House Publishers, for your vision and support for this book: Bob Hawkins, Aaron Dillon, Sherri Slopianka, Shann Hartley, Terry Glaspey, Ken Lorenz, Kathy Zemper, and Brad Moses.

Most of all, I am grateful to Jesus, the ultimate example of a relational, loving leader.

Contents

Preface

What are "essential habits"? Essential habits are those habits that are most necessary for healthy relational leadership. I have chosen essential habits like empathetic listening, comforting, and forgiveness as necessary for leading relationally at home, work, and in friendships, but I have not addressed other important ideas like how to lead a meeting or hire and fire personnel. Essential habits are necessary for leadership—without them, we cannot lead well.

One definition demands another. A "relational leader" is a leader who values relationships because humans are created in God's image. Humans deserve and expect love, respect, and accountability. A leader who values people knows the names of those who serve in her organization. She knows their spouses' and children's names. She knows what motivates her colleagues: money, recognition, time off, etc. She knows what makes her husband and children feel loved: affirmation, service, gifts, quality time, or affection. She knows the dreams and fears of those she leads, because she values people.

There is a real risk that a relational leader will be taken advantage of or even betrayed. Jesus had 12 disciples, and one of them was in it for the money and prestige—eventually he betrayed Jesus. In fact, Jesus saw it coming and exposed Judas the night of the Last Supper as the one who would betray Him. Better to have a relationship with your enemy and keep an eye on him than to have no relationship and be ambushed unexpectedly.

Essential Habits of Relational Leaders is a nonexhaustive, practical approach to creating and sustaining good habits that are necessary for leading others in a relational manner. Some of these ideas you may have tried before but then abandoned, others you may use and benefit from already, and a few may be new ways to better lead your coworkers, family, church volunteers, friends, or any other group that requires relational direction. Hopefully, you can improve on concepts you discover in this book and apply them to your situation.

Henri Nouwen, in his masterpiece *In the Name of Jesus*, describes a relational leader's heart, and offers us a fitting summons:

> Somehow we have come to believe that good leadership requires a safe distance from those we are called to lead. Medicine, psychiatry, and social work all offer us models in which "service" takes place in a one-way direction. But how can we lay down our life for those with whom we are not even allowed to enter into a deep, personal relationship? Laying down your life means making your own faith and doubt, hope and despair, joy and sadness, courage and fear available to others as ways of getting in touch with the Lord of life.[1]

My prayer is that all who read this book will find courage to answer the call to lay down our lives in acts of relational leadership.

Introduction:
Essential Habits of a Relational
Leader—an Example

*A generous man will prosper; he who refreshes
others will himself be refreshed.*

PROVERBS 11:25

The traffic was snarled on a rainy Friday night in Atlanta. Already fatigued from a full week of work, why would my wife, Rita, and I get back into the car and drive 90 minutes, bumper to bumper, into Buckhead? The relational investment one man and his family has made in me and my family over the past 30 years motivated me to honor Charlie on his 75th birthday. An intimate group of immediate family and close friends gathered to laugh, cry, and affirm the one who brought relational richness into their lives.

I watched and reflected as toasts began to flow like a dammed-up river of delight, bursting forth with refreshing force. A widow wept gracefully, "Charlie you were the coast guard for me when Sam died." A grandchild gushed in gratitude, "Pop, you and MeMe were there for me when my mom died, I'll never forget how you cared for me." Four children beamed in admiration and love for a dad who loved each of them uniquely, while friends pontificated on how they felt special because of the nature of their relationship with Charlie. I was honored to give a prayer of thanks to God for a life so well invested. Relational leaders invest in good habits today, so that they will be successful tomorrow.

Relational leadership cannot be bought, only sought. A relational leader is a person who first looks to give, not get, listen, not talk, serve, and not be served. The riches of relational wealth are realized as we recognize how valuable people are. They are created in the image of God for the purposes of God. When we place a high value on people, we treat them with respect and love. As Paul tells Timothy: "Command them to *do good, to be rich in good deeds, and to be generous and willing to share.* In this way they will lay up treasure for themselves as a firm foundation for the coming age, so they may take hold of the life that is truly life" (1 Timothy 6:18-19, emphasis added). Showing respect and love can be as simple as being on time for a meeting or as creative as collecting shared memories in a photo album.

Relational leaders are able to see others as the Lord sees them—with great potential to grow into who they are meant to be. A person's stock may be out of favor, but when they are down is when they need someone to believe in them and offer future hope beyond their fears. They need to hear the words of Proverbs: "There is surely a future hope for you, and your hope will not be cut off" (Proverbs 23:18). When we show interest in a person who is at their lowest of lows, we have more upside to one day celebrate. We refresh others as we help restore them back to God's original intent for their lives. The fulfillment of seeing a friend back into good graces with Christ is life that is truly life.

Essential Habits of Relational Leaders is about helping others find purpose and, in the process, fulfill our own. We grow to give instead of get, listen instead of talk, help instead of be helped, and offer introductions instead of seeking introductions. Our life purpose is fulfilled when we can help another fulfill their life purpose. Our time investment may be as simple as offering a prayer for wisdom or as significant as a job introduction that leads to a friend being hired. Learning to be a relational leader is looking out for the interests of others above our own—it is about being others-centered.

This book is for those who are tired of the old and shallow networking techniques and tactics that leave people feeling used and abused. I offer a fresh look at how to add value to relationships by seeking to understand someone's felt needs. That need could be for a job, but I also want to teach you how to help others discover a subtle, more important need, like becoming a more compassionate and engaged husband, wife, or parent. We are becoming relational leaders when we model for others how to connect people to the Lord, His resources, and to each other.

Chapter One

Grow Relational Capacity

Ignoring our emotions is turning our back on reality.
Listening to our emotions ushers us into reality. And reality
is where we meet God...Emotions are the language of
the soul. They are the cry that gives the heart a voice.

PETER SCAZZERO

Jesus Gets to the Heart of the Matter

Love is the most powerful weapon in the arsenal of a relational leader. Trust is the fruit of leaders who love well. Like the tip of an arrow, love points us to the bull's-eye of God. Love commandeers all other graces to engage the Lord's affection and His eternal concerns. When Jesus defined love as the greatest command, He gave us a glimpse into what He wants for the world and His children. A person motivated by love is only limited by her capacity to love the Lord and be loved by the Lord. Love is a muscle we exercise so that it will grow in stamina and strength. Jesus starts with the heart in His sequence of how we can love God: "Love the Lord your God with all your heart" (Mark 12:30). A relational leader's capacity to connect with other hearts is contingent on the health and capacity of her heart to care.

Love God with Your Emotions

Jesus starts at the heart of the matter—our heart. What captures our passions and yearnings? Our heart is the seat of our feelings and affections. We are drawn to what we desire—what we value. Yes, the heart follows what it treasures above all else. In the same way an engaged couple aggressively seeks each other's heart, so as the bride of Christ we passionately pursue His heart. As our heart loves Jesus, He simultaneously settles and stirs our emotions.

> **TAKEAWAY:** *Relational leaders cultivate love for God and a heart to love others with God.*

Relational Leaders Seek Ways to Grow Their Relational Capacity

Relational capacity is our ability to love others well out of the overflow of our relationship with the Lord. A creek has a limited flow of water, but the mighty Mississippi connects commerce across our great land. If we serve in our own strength, we can quickly lapse into a loveless routine void of the Spirit's inner strength and power. Our emotions become frazzled and unruly without God's grace, which, like a spiritual IV, nourishes our faith and love. We are wise to grow our capacity for relationships by being emotionally healthy.

What Does It Mean to Be Emotionally Healthy?

People who are emotionally healthy understand their flaws and accept their imperfections and their need for God's grace and forgiveness. Because they embrace their need for God's grace and forgiveness, they are able to extend the same grace and forgiveness to other people. Emotionally healthy individuals take captive their thoughts, understand their feelings, and control their behavior. When facing life's challenges, they become better, not bitter. They learn to process pain so that it does not fester and produce relational conflict. Emotionally healthy people love God and know that they are loved by God, and so are able to love for God.

Introvert or Extrovert

My tendency is to be an introvert, but in a professional capacity I have adjusted over the years to an extrovert approach when working with teams or getting to know people in social settings. Extroverts thrive on being with people, but they have to guard against being "an inch deep and a mile wide." Many times, the quality of our relationships determines the quality of our life, so we are wise to go deeper with a few people and enjoy the fruit of really knowing one another. If you are more of an introvert, stretch yourself by learning new relational skills like asking good questions and listening to understand. If you are an extrovert, consider a "less is more" approach in your attempt to meet new people.

> **Point to Ponder:** Introverts and extroverts have the potential to increase their relational capacity.

A Caring Community Who Lovingly Calls Us Out

I am learning to defer to my wife, Rita, when someone in our community group of six couples (we have met regularly for eight years) asks us how our marriage is. I tend to say we are "doing great," but I may be out of sync with the condition of my wife's heart. Recently, we were asked this caring question and my sweetie bravely stated, "I don't feel like I am being heard by Boyd." I was humbled. My first instinct (not a healthy one) was to justify, defend, and rationalize as my ego and pride do not like to be called out. Fortunately, restrained by the Spirit, I listened as she explained my insensitivity, and our caring friends instructed me in how to better engage with Rita's heart. To process our pain, it takes other people who provide us with a safe environment.

> **Point to Ponder:** We are better together; by ourselves we drift into emotional self-deception.

Emotional Health Incubates in a Heart Guarded by God's Peace

The condition of our heart is an indicator of our emotional health. A wounded heart limps along vulnerable to fatigue and frustration, while a healed heart can resist the wiles of the world. "Above all else, guard your heart, for everything you do flows from it" (Proverbs 4:23).

Healthy emotions heal. A strong heart has access to an abundance of grace, so its capacity to offer forgiveness and exercise patience is vast.

Yes, the grace of God gives health and wellness to all who engage it. When our emotions are in good shape, we are in sync with the Spirit.

Just as we care for our physical health, so must we manage our emotional well-being. Checkups with a mature Jesus follower increase our understanding of our emotional state. The expertise of a trusted spiritual advisor is necessary for us to be objective in our own emotional assessment. Like a trainer who teaches how to keep our body healthy with a balance of weight training and cardio, so a spiritual trainer gives us insights in how to express our feelings and forgive offenses.

Point to Ponder: *Emotional healthcare requires time and attention in the same way we care for our bodies.*

The Holy Spirit is the best manager of our emotions. Just as a successful coach leads a team to work together to win, so the Spirit leads our emotions to work together for God's glory. When our emotions are under the influence of the Holy Spirit, we walk in wholeness and holiness. The Spirit helps us filter our feelings, leaving us more emotionally healthy. The Spirit removes distasteful impurities. A heart controlled by the Spirit is able to give life to others.

Are you keenly sensitive to the Spirit's leading or are you overly sensitive to fleshly feelings? Have your emotional wounds healed? Take a risk and be vulnerable about your past hurts so you can experience healing. As Isaiah says, "The LORD will guide you always; He will satisfy your needs in a sun-scorched land and will strengthen your frame. You will be like a well-watered garden, like a spring whose waters never fail" (Isaiah 58:11). Surround yourself with caring Christ followers with whom you can process your feelings. Most of all, share your heart with your Savior, Jesus, who will cleanse, heal, and make your heart whole! As Paul puts it, "the peace of God, which transcends all understanding, will guard your hearts and your minds in Christ Jesus" (Philippians 4:7).

TAKEAWAY: *Relational leaders experience the peace of God when God is the protector of their heart and mind.*

Relational Leaders Are Emotionally Healthy

Steve is a friend I met at a leadership conference in 1994 who was able to "retire" at age 54 and volunteer his time to help people manage their money wisely. A former orthodontist, he was as passionate about people straightening out their financial lives as he had been straightening teeth! For seven years, we traveled the Southeast and beyond to train and coach leaders in how to facilitate small-group Bible studies on money. My life is much richer today because of Steve's ability to share common-sense solutions to the issues I faced as a 30-something-year-old. For me, he is a model of how to keep serving the kingdom after "retirement." Because Steve was emotionally and financially heathy, he was able to energetically serve others.

> **Point to Ponder:** When we have more time to give back, we need to be at our emotional best.

Healthy Hearts Bring Relational Healing and Wholeness

As you begin to experience the freedom of loving the Lord wholeheartedly and being loved by Him, you will become a channel of healing for others who hunger to be relationally healthy. Prepare your heart in prayer, and the Spirit will position you to love others well. Out of the overflow of your relationship with Jesus you will experience healthy relationships with others. Growing one's capacity for relationships is an essential habit of relational leaders.

> **TAKEAWAY:** When relational leaders understand and engage their emotions, they are able to connect with others' hearts.

Summary of Chapter One Takeaways

1. Relational leaders cultivate love for God and a heart to love others with God.

2. Relational leaders experience the peace of God when God is the protector of their heart and mind.

3. When relational leaders understand and engage their emotions, they are able to connect with others' hearts.

Chapter Two

Restore a Relationship When Trust Is Broken

Brethren, if any person is overtaken in misconduct or sin of any sort, you who are spiritual [who are responsive to and controlled by the Spirit] should set him right and restore and reinstate him, without any sense of superiority and with all gentleness, keeping an attentive eye on yourself, lest you should be tempted also.

GALATIANS 6:1 AMPC

The work of restoration cannot begin until a problem is fully faced.

DAN ALLENDER

Not Another Business Meeting

Our 17-year-old daughter blurted out to me in frustration, "Dad, every time we talk, it feels like a business meeting." I had overdrawn my emotional equity with my teenager. I had become hyper-controlling and hyper-fearful because of a teenage boy I did not like. In my mind, he was suspect—suspect for not looking me in the eyes, suspect for the distasteful way he dressed, suspect because his family showered my little girl with gifts I could not afford. He was suspect because he dismissed my question about his plan to stay pure with my daughter. I was stressed out.

Nonetheless, I knew in my heart that I needed to adjust my overbearing approach to my sweet and sensitive girl, or our relationship was about to go completely off the rails. We needed relational restoration because our trust in each other had grown weak (if it was not broken already). After conferring with my wise wife and asking the Lord for my heart and mind to be motivated by love and not fear, I had a new idea. Instead of obsessing over my worry, I focused on an activity my daughter loved.

"What if we take scuba diving lessons together?" Her response told me I'd chosen the right path: "That sounds so fun! Thank you, Dad!" By God's grace I began to build back trust with my daughter by trusting her to follow Jesus, to make wise choices, and to honor me. Once I took my eyes off myself and the selfish fears of my image being tainted, I was able to trust the Lord with my girl!

Point to Ponder: *Relational trust can be rebuilt by initiating trust in others.*

We spent the summer showing up for weekly scuba classes. As we progressed, I felt my stamina wane. Like a baby salmon swimming upstream, I felt the physical challenge of the training acutely. But it was a small price to pay for replacing my business-meeting approach with a caring, relational approach. My daughter went on to be certified, while a sinus infection torpedoed my certification dive in Florida. August rolled around, and our pastor began a series called the "Power of the Path," about how our direction determines our destination.

Three weeks into the sermon series, my discerning daughter said to my wife and me, "God really spoke to me at church today. I am on the wrong path dating Chip (not his real name). I plan to break off our relationship immediately." "Yes" we blurted out, "sounds like the wise thing to do." Chip did not take no for an answer, and it was all I could do to not step in and interpret to him what *no* meant. And yet, our bold baby girl stood her ground, even to his pushy mom. Afterward, the Lord sent my daughter the love of her life. Rules are necessary to protect and preserve, but relationships flourish best in a loving environment. Creativity needed to replace my repetitive business meetings!

TAKEAWAY: *Relational leaders understand that rules are necessary to protect and preserve, but relationships flourish best in a loving environment.*

How to Restore a Relationship When Trust Is Broken

If I could sit down with you and have an honest conversation about your relationships, I bet you could tell me a story about a time when someone took advantage of you, betrayed you, or let you down. Perhaps they failed to give you the love for which you long or the support you desire. As a result, trust was broken. Or, perhaps you were the one who contributed to the death of trust through some sinful attitude or action. The good news is that the Bible gives a prescription for the restoration of relationships. In Matthew, Jesus says the following: "Therefore, if you are offering your gift at the altar and there remember that your brother or sister has something against you, leave your gift there in front of the altar. First, go and be reconciled to them; then come and offer your gift" (Matthew 5:23-25). The prescription is to go. That sounds challenging, but it is not impossible! Go. Admit you're wrong. Be reconciled.

When trust is broken, restoring it takes more than an apology. Why? Because the beginning of reconciliation happens with an apology or a request for forgiveness, but total relational healing happens when trust is restored, and that often takes more than an "I'm sorry."

> **Point to Ponder:** When trust is broken, restoration is not always as quick and simple as an apology.

Relational healing happens when both parties forgive, of course, but also when the offender moves from "I'm sorry" to action. They are willing to do what is necessary to make the one they have offended or hurt feel safe. If that means the offending party needs to tell their mate where they are going after work and call home at noon, they'll do it. If it means they need to submit themselves to counsel or accountability, they'll do it. If it means they need to take a class or have some hard conversations to regain trust, they'll do it.

When we are serious about relational restoration, we'll be truly remorseful about the sin we have committed against our brother or sister in Christ, and we'll move from "I'm sorry" to action. We will be willing not only to ask for forgiveness but to do the work that is necessary for healing to take place.

When there is consistency between words and actions, between intention and behavior, trust can be restored. And when two people work together to restore trust, great things happen. Intimacy grows. Joy increases. And God is glorified. There is no relationship that is so broken that God cannot restore it when both parties humble themselves and work together to restore trust.

Is there a relationship in your life that has been broken because trust has been broken? How can you contribute to the restoration of trust? And, if you are the one in the wrong, are you willing to humble yourself and do the work to restore confidence and trust? Are you willing to help your brother or sister in Christ feel safe with you again?

> **TAKEAWAY:** *Relational leaders humble themselves and work with others to restore trust.*

Jesus's Rejection Became Our Means of Restoration

A few men, green with envy, branded Jesus and His followers as power-hungry political fanatics. However, heaven did not sit still in the face of these false accusations. "The stone the builders rejected has become the cornerstone; the Lord has done this, and it is marvelous in our eyes" (Mark 12:10-11). The One whose character was assassinated and whose body was crucified became the payment for His critics' sin. We can reject Jesus as our Savior, but belief in Him is still required for a right relationship with God.

> *Point to Ponder: After God restores us to Himself, our soul craves Christ's company.*

When we accept Christ, He brings us back to God. Our arrogant intellect rejected the existence of a personal God, but since He restored us to Himself, we crave His company. Our self-reliant spirit dismissed dependency on the Almighty, but now we are strengthened in Him.

Our drive to accomplish ignored grace, but now, having tasted God's grace, we hunger for more. Our pride looked down on spiritual people, but now our humility compels us to look up to heaven for help!

Be a restorer of relationships, not a rejecter of relationships. Ask yourself: what relationship needs your time and attention in order to be rebuilt? We are the Lord's ministers of reconciliation. Christ is the capstone of our character, and we have the honor of laying His cornerstone of convictions in the lives of our children and grandchildren. Invite those who have rejected Jesus to accept Him. As Scripture says, "If you return to the Almighty, you will be restored" (Job 22:23). Like a refurbished piece of furniture, His restoration is beautiful!

> **TAKEAWAY:** *Relational leaders are the Lord's ministers of reconciliation.*

Summary of Chapter Two Takeaways

1. Relational leaders understand that rules are necessary to protect and preserve, but relationships flourish best in a loving environment.

2. Relational leaders humble themselves and work with others to restore trust.

3. Relational leaders are the Lord's ministers of reconciliation.

Chapter Three

Avoid the Relationship Killer

A gentle answer turns away wrath,
but a harsh word stirs up anger.

PROVERBS 15:1

Angry people are not always wise.

JANE AUSTEN

Anger Is Toxic to Relationships

Anger is toxic to relationships. It seems to come out of nowhere and wreck relationships. But does it really come out of nowhere? In an instant, a conversation can shift to a defensive, detrimental tone because anger is released like a wasp's nest smashed by an intrusive shoe on its camouflaged burrow. Poisonous are the stings, causing an allergic reaction of unrighteousness. The best remedy is an injection of humility to contain the reddened, swelling of pride. As James writes, "My dear brothers and sisters, take note of this: Everyone should be quick to listen, slow to speak and slow to become angry, because human anger does not produce the righteousness that God desires. Therefore, get rid of all moral filth and the evil that is so prevalent and humbly accept the word planted in you, which can save you" (James 1:19-21).

> **Point to Ponder:** Anger is toxic to relationships.

Paul gives clear instructions on how to prevent pride from pouncing on people who want to avoid human anger and embrace what God desires—righteousness. "Get rid of all bitterness, rage, and anger, brawling and slander, along with every form of malice. Be kind and compassionate to one another, forgiving each other, just as in Christ God forgave you" (Ephesians 4:31-32). A posture of patient listening is a highly effective deterrent to the destructiveness of anger. Instead of reacting defensively ("The reason I said what I said was..."), respond empathetically: "I'm sorry, it sounds like you feel really hurt." Anger should be rejected and replaced with patient listening. Put off pride and instead, live out the humble word which is planted in our hearts (Psalm 119:11), our salvation from anger's harshness.

Are you sometimes ambushed by anger, unable to see it coming? Perhaps you react in the moment with heightened emotions in a high-pitched voice and are instantly ashamed of your actions. If you regularly find yourself seeming calm on the surface but simmering underneath, you can dig up the roots of pride with the shovel of humility. Identify the reasons for your anger: fatigue, rejection, feeling hurt, or not getting your way. Instead of holding on to your hurt, release it with mercy and forgiveness. Speak forgiveness to another or ask for forgiveness when you need it.

Be careful not to justify your anger by thinking it is righteous; reserve this lofty designation for the Lord's anger. Anger on earth most often has its origins in human sinfulness. Grace extends the fuse of your frustrations, so you do not easily blow up and ruin relationships. Kindness deflects the blow of harshness, and patience eliminates disrespect from your conversations. Like hearty Zoysia grass overtakes weeds, the good fruit of the Spirit is able to replace the bad fruit of angry actions. Like Paul says, "You were taught, with regard to your former way of life, to put off your old self, which is being corrupted by its deceitful desires; to be made new in the attitude of your minds; and to put on the new self, created to be like God in true righteousness and holiness" (Ephesians 4:22-24). Confess anger as a toxic agent in your relationships and process it with patient love and listening.

TAKEAWAY: *Relational leaders are slow to call their anger righteous. They reserve this lofty designation for the Lord's anger.*

A Friend Full of Joyful Praise

I really enjoy the company of my friend Mike. He seems to always look for the things in life to be joyful about, and he lets go of things out of his control. Even though I know he has his share of relational challenges, financial hurdles to overcome, and family dynamics to manage, he keeps his focus on finding favor with his heavenly Father. Mike replaces pride and anger with humility and joy. My friend knows the secret of being content with much or little as he rests in Christ's acceptance and approval.

Because my colleague has such strong self-awareness and God-awareness, he has the capacity for the "joy of the Lord to be his strength." Joy is the overflow of learning to love like Jesus, contagious and comforting—joy brings out the best in others and brings a smile to their face. People look forward to seeing joy coming!

> **Point to Ponder:** Joyful praise reflects God's presence and is pleasant to be around.

Anger's Enemy

Hurtful emotional outbursts overwhelm any evidence of love's presence. However, anger's most feared enemy is love and forgiveness. Love can handle anger's influence. "Love is not easily angered" (1 Corinthians 13:5). A loving person sees anger coming and prepares for its onslaught with a prayer for patience and forgiveness. When we build our relationships on a foundation of love, it becomes possible to moderate our tempers. Love does not allow anger to make itself at home in a heart that's been hurt. It avoids anger.

Often, the people who know us the best hurt us the most. As a result, it can be hard to love them because our pain impels us to retaliate. This is when we must seek the Lord for an infusion of His fresh fire of love and forgiveness. We need unconditional love the most during times when our spirit has been crushed by an unloving person. Let go of the need to inflict pain on the one who was insensitive to you. Grace and forgiveness are tools of love that rebuild broken relationships. Do to others as you would have them do to you. As Jesus says, "If you love those who love you, what credit is that to you? Even sinners love those who love them. And if you do good to those who are good to you, what credit is that to you? Even sinners do that" (Luke 6:32-33).

Your love is a gift you can give in place of angry reaction. Rise above petty arguments and model a mature faith that doesn't fight back in raw irritation. Because you have been loved supremely by your Savior, lavish the same unrestricted love on those who let you down. Replace an angry attack on your adversary with patient restraint. Love much because you have been forgiven much by God.

Let the Lord's love alleviate you from the need to be right. Dismiss the need to get your own way and meet your loved one at their point of need. Apply the ancient ointment of love to disjointed, even diseased, relationships. Remove the cancer of anger with the sharp scalpel of self-less love. The Lord's love frees your heart to be a fierce lover for Him!

TAKEAWAY: Relational leaders are not demanding but instead give room for flexibility and restoration.

Avoid Friendships with Angry People

What's behind a short-fused temper? Why do some people fly off in a rage for ridiculous reasons? A hot-tempered person brings out the worst in everyone. Anger comes from angst in the soul. It is the expression of a faith-starved heart. Mistreatment, abandonment, rejection, and loss all contribute to anger. Because anger is unappealing, it is wise to avoid the angry, lest you become like them. As Proverbs says, "Do not make friends with a hot-tempered person, do not associate with one easily angered" (Proverbs 22:24). There is no worse feeling than being trapped in the downward spiral of fury and rage. Anger is unattractive, unprofitable, and immature. Resentful people are sucked into a cycle of self-pity and self-indulgence. Service is their secret to freedom.

Point to Ponder: *Anger comes from angst in the soul. It is the expression of a faith-starved heart.*

We must not be intimidated by the angry. We must not fear the fury of the unfaithful. Moses learned this lesson: "By faith he left Egypt, not fearing the king's anger; he persevered because he saw Him who is invisible" (Hebrews 11:27). Begin by faith to put this irritating individual in God's hands. God can handle them. Do not try to change the angry, for they will only increase in anger. Instead, intercede to Christ on their behalf for His patience and forgiveness to fill their soul. Angry hearts can only be healed by grace.

If anger controls your actions, repent and ask Jesus to set you free. An angry disposition is a veil of unresolved sin. "Everyone should be quick to listen, slow to speak and slow to become angry, for man's anger does not bring about the righteous life that God desires" (James 1:19b-20). Let the Lord love on you and draw you unto His mercy. The Lord loves you and forgives you. He understands the proper use of anger. Ask Christ to channel your energy into eternal initiatives like building a church, feeding the poor, and serving your family. Be an activist for Almighty God.

TAKEAWAY: *Relational leaders avoid a disposition of anger through mutual forgiveness.*

Summary of Chapter Three Takeaways

1. Relational leaders are slow to call their anger righteous. They reserve this lofty designation for the Lord's anger.

2. Relational leaders are not demanding but instead give room for flexibility and restoration.

3. Relational leaders avoid a disposition of anger through mutual forgiveness.

Chapter Four

Work Through Relational Conflict

Never hold a grudge or try to get even, but plan your life around the noblest way to benefit others. Do your best to live as everybody's friend. Beloved, don't be obsessed with taking revenge, but leave that to God's righteous justice. For the Scriptures say: "If you don't take justice in your own hands, I will release justice for you," says the Lord. And: If your enemy is hungry, buy him lunch! Win him over with kindness. For your surprising generosity will awaken his conscience, and God will reward you with favor. Never let evil defeat you, but defeat evil with good.

ROMANS 12:17-21 THE PASSION BIBLE

Peace is not absence of conflict, it is the ability to handle conflict by peaceful means.

RONALD REAGAN

How to Handle Relational Conflict

There comes a time in every relationship when conflict occurs. Sometimes it's been brewing for a while and then erupts. Other times, it comes out of nowhere. When conflict happens, you can either solve conflict God's way, or you can mismanage the conflict and destroy relational intimacy. As Paul says, "Bless those who persecute you; bless and do not curse them" (Romans 12:14).

Do Not Return Offense for Offense

When the other person becomes offended by something you did, said, or didn't do, a natural response is to return offense for offense rather than respond in humility. When this happens, you can allow the offense you feel to determine how you respond. But this never leads to conflict resolution. Choose humility and grace instead.

It's natural when we're angry to want to let someone "have it" by lashing out with angry, cutting, or insulting words. You may be tempted to bring up offenses from the past, use passive-aggressive language, shame the other person, cut down their character, or try to manipulate them to get what you want. But these tactics never lead to conflict resolution. They will only destroy the relationship. As Peter exhorts us, "Do not repay evil with evil or insult with insult. On the contrary, repay evil with blessing, because to this you were called so that you may inherit a blessing" (1 Peter 3:9).

Do Not Run Away

Some people enjoy sparring; others loathe conflict and even find it terrifying. For this reason, some folks want to "run away" from conflict by shutting down and refusing to talk it out. Or, they may even go to an extreme and end the relationship or cut the other person off without seeking to solve the conflict. This will not lead to the intimacy you desire.

Point to Ponder: *Every meaningful relationship will be tested by conflict.*

Let Go of Grudges

Some folks may say they accept an apology, but in reality, they are still holding a grudge. If you keep rehearsing what the other person did to you, call your friends over and over and repeat what happened, even though the conflict has been long over, while saying you are "fine" to the person with whom you are having the conflict, this will also ruin your relationship.

To conduct relationships in a two-faced or duplicitous way never leads to peace. To truly forgive, process through your pain, seek resolution with the other person, but don't nurse a grudge. To handle conflict God's way and not cooperate with the devil's agenda for your relationships takes courage, humility, love, and confidence. You have to trust that God sees and knows and that He will help you do what is right. Choose to handle conflict in a holy way, even if the other person does not. You'll be glad you did.

Lord, when conflict happens in my life, please give me the wisdom to handle it Your way and not to cooperate with the devil's plans. Amen.

TAKEAWAY: Relational leaders must love peace in order to make peace.

How Conflict Can Improve Relationships

Not long ago, I experienced an unexpected conflict with someone I desired to know better but who was only an acquaintance. When the conflict unexpectedly erupted due to a misunderstanding, at first I was hurt, and then I was angry.

But before I responded in an ungodly way, I remembered something very important: conflict can be leveraged to improve relational intimacy. As Proverbs says, "A person's wisdom yields patience; it is to one's glory to overlook an offense" (Proverbs 19:11). You see, during every conflict there is a moment when you first become hurt or angry and you feel like giving back the hurt you have received. At this moment, you are standing at a relational crossroads: you can go one way toward greater relational intimacy or another way toward relational destruction. You can wisely use the conflict to grow your relationship or you can mismanage it and allow it to ruin your relationship. Follow Peter's advice: "Do not repay evil with evil or insult with insult. On the contrary, repay evil with blessing, because to this you were called so that you may inherit a blessing" (1 Peter 3:9).

Point to Ponder: Conflict processed well can lead to a more intimate relationship.

If you want to build intimacy in your relationship and use conflict to become a catalyst to become closer with another person, here are some things you can do:

Recognize and Empathize with Another's Hurt

When the other person is upset and perhaps even blaming you for something you didn't do, it's easy to become offended and respond in kind. But do not allow your ungodly emotions to rule you. Instead, listen to their heart behind their words, because behind hurtful words, there is often a hurting person who is upset because they haven't received something they want. Perhaps they want your understanding, your time, your help, or your love. Maybe they feel shoved aside, ignored, taken advantage of, or devalued.

Respond with Understanding and Comfort

Even if you are not guilty of what they are accusing you of and they have misunderstood you, listen to their heart as they speak. Don't respond to their tone. Then, minister to their hurt by acknowledging it with words of grace. "I am sorry I hurt you." Remember, the point is not that you are right and they are wrong. The point of resolving the conflict is reconciliation, extending grace, and allowing the other person to see Christ in you. When you apologize, you are not admitting you did what they are accusing you of; you are simply acknowledging their pain. You are saying, "I see you and I care." Once you have acknowledged their pain, ask them if there is anything else they need to let you know or ask them to tell you more about how they feel.

Adjust to Meet Another's Expectations

If you know someone needs something from you and it is within your power to do so, give them what they want. For example, if your mate says they are upset because you are always late picking them up from work and that makes them feel devalued, tell them you will do your best to be on time. Then make a genuine effort to do that very thing. A willingness to change for the greater good of a relationship reveals a heart of love and sacrifice. An unwillingness to change shows our deepest selfishness. When conflict brings up the need to change, love the other person by giving them what they need (except in abusive situations).

The next time you have a conflict in your life, choose the high road. Choose God's humble way. And even though you may feel like lashing out, don't allow your emotions to dictate your actions or words. Instead, allow grace to determine what you say and do. You won't regret reaching out to mend a fractured friendship.

TAKEAWAY: *For the sake of peace, relational leaders do not compromise work culture or home culture.*

Peacemakers Are Peace-Loving

"The wisdom that comes from heaven is first of all pure; then *peace-loving*, considerate, submissive, full of mercy and good fruit, impartial and sincere" (James 3:17).

There are some things you can avoid in life. You can avoid long lines at the bookstore; just purchase what you want to read online. You can avoid eating a pile of cookies; just don't buy them. You can avoid getting trick-or-treaters; you can just leave the house on the evening of October 31. But there are some things in life that you just can't avoid, no matter how much you don't like them. Conflict is one of those things. It comes knocking on everyone's front door at some time or another and it isn't polite. It just comes right in and sits down on the couch. And, when that happens, you have two choices: you can allow it to stay and really make a mess of your life and emotions, or you can handle it God's way and experience peace.

When I was growing up, I really disliked conflict. I was a middle child and my mantra was, "Why can't we all just get along?" I did everything I could to solve conflict with others, which often included trying to avoid the problem by being extra nice. As you can imagine, this didn't work. It wasn't until I was in my late twenties that I learned that my avoidance tactics didn't help at all. All they did was make me feel like an insecure victim who was afraid of people, and that made other people uncomfortable. I did not understand that peacemaking and avoiding are not the same thing. While avoiding is passive, peacemaking is often proactive. Peacemakers are willing to make the first move toward the person with whom they are having the conflict.

> **Point to Ponder:** *Peacemakers are proactive, unafraid to make the first move to repair a relationship.*

Peacemaking is difficult. Who likes to have that hard conversation or that difficult meeting? Who likes to be the one who initiates when it is much easier to retreat and hope the whole mess goes away? No one. But the wise person knows that conflict usually doesn't resolve itself. They know that if they refuse to settle the conflict they will personally suffer because they won't experience peace. And, they also know they will be blessed if they attempt to make peace. As Jesus said, "Blessed are the peacemakers, for they will be called children of God" (Matthew 5:9).

Peacemakers are not just blessed because they obey God's command to make peace. They are also blessed because the peace they create always comes rolling back to them, filling up their hearts. Holding on to offenses and grudges does the exact opposite. Bitterness and anger have no benefits. There is absolutely no blessing in not handling conflict—or handling it in the wrong way.

Peacemaking takes self-control. Peacemaking requires that I do not open my mouth and spout off meanness in response to meanness (1 Peter 3:9). Instead, it takes maturity to hold your tongue or keep your fingers off the computer keyboard when you would rather shoot back a snarky response. "A gentle answer turns away wrath, but a harsh word stirs up anger" (Proverbs 15:1). Peacemaking requires courage. Peacemaking necessitates wisdom. Peacemaking is born of maturity. Be that person. Not just for the other person, but for God—and for yourself. You'll be glad you did.

Lord, help me to be a peacemaker. I want to experience
your peace in my life, I want to please you and I

want to be a blessing. Give me the courage and the
wisdom I need to solve conflict Your way. Amen.

TAKEAWAY: Relational leaders set a peaceful tone and tenor in their conversations.

Summary of Chapter Four Takeaways

1. Relational leaders must love peace in order to make peace.
2. For the sake of peace, relational leaders do not compromise work culture or home culture.
3. Relational leaders set a peaceful tone and tenor in their conversations.

Chapter Five

Nurture Past Relationships

*A dear friend will love you no matter what, and a
family sticks together through all kinds of trouble.*

PROVERBS 17:17 THE PASSION TRANSLATION

*If you live to be 100, I hope I live to be 100 minus
1 day, so I never have to live without you.*

WINNIE THE POOH

Friendships Are a Stewardship

Charlie, whose seventy-fifth birthday I described in the introduction,
is by far the best nurturer of old friendships I have ever met. He
called me a few years ago to pray for a high school friend of his, Pete, who
was dying of cancer. I was not surprised to learn that Charlie had already
driven four hours the day before to be at the bedside of his childhood
friend. Being a friend means being responsible—friendships require
good stewardship. Relationships are God's gift to us, and God requires us
to manage them well for Him. Friendships originating with the Divine
are divine and deserve our life-long attention and intentionality.

> **Point to Ponder:** Friendships originating with the Divine are
> divine and deserve our life-long attention and intentionality.

Relational Leaders Experience Sworn Friendships

Jonathan said to David, "Go in peace, for we have sworn friendship
with each other in the name of the LORD" (1 Samuel 20:42). Friendship
sworn in the name of the Lord is based on faith. Friendship loyalty, when
based on relationship and commitment to the Lord, is an extremely

strong bond for friends. There is no wavering of commitment when Christ is central to the friendship. This is what a sworn friendship is. When friendship is based on the Lord, the friends take on the Lord's attitude toward friendship. The Lord sticks closer than a brother. He never leaves or forsakes His friends. Jesus personified friendship as He served His friends, forgave His friends, loved, taught, rebuked, prayed, and gave to His friends.

Sworn friendship is committed, especially during dire circumstances. Friends who have sworn friendship to each other have made a commitment to always be there for the other person. Sworn friends seek out the very best for each other during hard times. These kinds of friendships require an exorbitant amount of time, money, and effort. They require lots of maintenance during times of crisis. The crisis situation may be of the friend's own doing, or a result of forces outside of his control. Your friend may be on the brink of bankruptcy because of poor financial decisions. You serve him even though he suffers from self-inflicted wounds. Your friend's health may be going downhill fast; if so, be there to listen.

Friends who commit to friendship in the name of the Lord defend you, even when it means risking other respected relationships. Faithful friends will stand up for you even when it costs them—it might cost them their job, a promotion, or financial security. They might risk being misunderstood. But, because they are invested in you unconditionally, these friends are honored to defend you, especially in your absence. They ask questions of your unseen critics such as, "Have you talked to them about this?" or "I'm surprised by what you say. There must be more to the story." Friends stick up for each other in the face of caustic critics. Love is not silent; it speaks up.

Friendships sworn in the name of the Lord last. These are not fair-weather friendships, but they last through the ups and the downs. Acquaintances fade away over time, but faithful friendships based on God last for a lifetime. Take an inventory of your friendships. Identify the ones built on God's principles and value them more. Be intentional in your investment of time with friendships sworn in the name of the

Lord. Do not take these special friendships for granted. Pray for them aggressively.

Above all else, cultivate your friendship with Christ. His model of friendship will raise the quality of your friendships. His friendship is forever. His friendship is immediately accessible. His friendship is honest and loving. His friendship is faithful.

Jesus spoke eloquently about friends: "Greater love has no one than this, that he lay down his life for his friends. You are my friends if you do what I command. I no longer call you servants, because a servant does not know his master's business. Instead, I have called you friends, for everything that I learned from my Father I have made known to you" (John 15:13-15).

Heavenly Father, grow me into a loyal friend who
defends and supports during difficult days.

TAKEAWAY: *Relational leaders value friendships based on their mutual friendship with Jesus.*

Lifelong Friendships Help Fulfill God's Purpose for Our Lives

"He who walks with wise men will be wise, but the companion of fools will suffer harm" (Proverbs 13:20 NASB). Mother Teresa said, "I can do things you cannot. You can do things I cannot; together we can do great things." These are wise words we see demonstrated in many lives in Scripture. Moses accomplished God's plan with the help of others; Nehemiah rallied helpers together to rebuild Jerusalem's wall; the disciples relied on one another, Paul relied on Timothy and Barnabas, and even Jesus was dependent on His Father.

Today, every pastor, football coach, disaster recovery leader, author, youth minister, company CEO, mother, and teacher accomplish the great things they do because they have supportive, servant-minded people standing with them who believe in their God-given mission.

Surrounding yourself with those who will pull you toward God's plan for your life and not away from it is critical. It's important to make friends with people who will celebrate what God is calling you to and who do not shame you or tell you what you believe God is asking you to do is not possible.

> **Point to Ponder:** I can do things you cannot. You can do things I cannot; together we can do great things.

In Numbers 13, the Lord told Moses to send some men out from the Israelite camp to spy on the land of Canaan, the land He was giving them, and to come back with a report. They did, and when they returned, they reported that the land was beautiful—just as God promised—but that there were giants already living there. They said, "the people who live there are powerful, and the cities are fortified and very large. We even saw descendants of Anak there. The Amalekites live in the Negev; the Hittites, Jebusites and Amorites live in the hill country; and the Canaanites live near the sea and along the Jordan" (Numbers 13:28-29).

But Caleb, who believed what God promised, said, "We should go up and take possession of the land, for we can certainly do it" (Numbers 13:30). But the naysayers who had gone on the mission said, in essence, "No way. They are stronger than we are. We are like grasshoppers compared to them" (cf. Numbers 13:31-33).

To make a long story short, the whole camp became very upset, and some of the people wished they had been left in Egypt. The Lord was displeased with their reaction. He said, "How long will these people treat me with contempt? How long will they refuse to believe in me, in spite of all the signs I have performed among them?" Can you imagine what would have happened if the Israelite spies had supported Moses because they believed the Lord? They would have been inspired to go and take the land God had promised. But instead, they were afraid and refused to do the tasks to which God had called them.

The example of the Israelite spies illustrates the importance of surrounding yourself with lifelong friends who believe in your God-given mission. You need the companionship of life-long friends to see great things happen. Nurture long-established relationships. When we do not take for granted long-standing relationships but instead appreciate them and draw strength from them, they enable us to walk in our calling and fulfill God's purposes.

> *Lord, give me the wisdom I need to surround myself with people who believe You and help me to trust You so that I am an encouragement to others as they fulfill their God-given purpose.*

TAKEAWAY: Relational leaders do not take friendships for granted; rather, they nurture them over the years.

Faithful Friends Leave an Influential Legacy Even After They Are Gone

I recently wept when a friend died. He was not a close friend, but a friend nonetheless. His life stood for decency, common sense, and compassion. I attended his funeral, and once again I was overcome by moments of emotion: joy for his friendship with Jesus and grief because he was gone. I was reminded by his death how much friends mean. When I lose someone, I seem to appreciate them even more. Faithful friends are a gift from God and are not to be taken for granted. "You are my friends if you do what I command. I no longer call you servants, because a servant does not know his master's business. Instead, I have called you friends, for everything that I learned from my Father I have made known to you" (John 15:14–15).

Point to Ponder: "Faithful friends are God's gift to us to help keep our friendship with Jesus growing."

Jesus describes as His friends those of us who love and obey Him. We are not just faceless servants obeying our master but are affectionately called friends by our Lord Christ. Many children who grow up in the faith learn well the meaning of that old song, "What a Friend We Have in Jesus." As we grow older as followers of Jesus, we are meant to keep this childlike expression of friendship with Jesus. He is our faithful friend, ever present to listen to us and to love us. "One who has unreliable friends soon comes to ruin, but there is a friend who sticks closer than a brother" (Proverbs 18:24).

Do your friends find you faithful, especially in their time of need? Perhaps there is a precious friend who needs your extra attention. In the past you have leaned on him, but now he needs your shoulder to cry on and your prayers to support him. Even the most solid Christian need not suffer alone. Or a friend may need a voice of reality to remind her where she came from. True friends do not shy away from being a loving truth teller. Faithful friends speak up, even at the risk of the relationship. By God's grace, a tested friendship grows into a stronger friendship.

Because of our companionship with Christ, He makes known to us His Father's heart. As the book of Job says, "My intercessor is my friend as my eyes pour out tears to God" (Job 16:20). If we want to know the will of our heavenly Father, we go to His Son Jesus and learn of Him. Because of our growing friendship with Christ, He continues to reveal to us the deep secrets of God. Like all relationships, the more we get to know one other, the more we understand each other. Every day with Jesus is sweeter than the day before, because we know our faithful friend a little bit better.

Heavenly Father, thank You for my faithful
friend, Savior, and Lord, Jesus Christ. Grow
me into a faithful friend to my friends.

TAKEAWAY: *Relational leaders understand that friendships tested by adversity can become stronger friendships.*

Summary of Chapter Five Takeaways

1. Relational leaders value friendships based on their mutual friendship with Jesus.

2. Relational leaders do not take friendships for granted; rather, they nurture them over the years.

3. Relational leaders understand that friendships tested by adversity can become stronger friendships.

Chapter Six

Know People and Be Known by People

Confess your sins to each other and pray for each other so that you may be healed. The prayer of a righteous person is powerful and effective.

JAMES 5:16

A person's name is to him or her the sweetest and most important sound in any language.

DALE CARNEGIE

Jesus Valued a Person's Name

What's in a name? The account of Peter's confession gives us some insight: "He said to them, 'But who do you say that I am?' Simon Peter replied, 'You are the Christ, the Son of the living God.' And Jesus answered him, 'Blessed are you, Simon Bar-Jonah! For flesh and blood has not revealed this to you, but my Father who is in heaven. And I tell you, you are Peter, and on this rock I will build my church, and the gates of hell shall not prevail against it'" (Matthew 16:15-18 ESV). Peter's confession of Jesus's identity invited Jesus to affirm how His heavenly Father had revealed this significant truth to Peter's open heart. Peter's correct interpretation became an opportunity for Jesus to teach about building His church. Jesus associated the meaning of the name Peter, or "rock," with the church, validating both Peter and the building of Christ's church. Jesus found significance in Peter's name and challenged Peter's commitment to His church.

A Boss Who Called Me Brother

I once had a boss who called me "brother" over my five-year employment. In Christian culture, this is an accepted manner to greet one another: "brother" for men and "sister" for women. But it is not often used as a substitute for someone's name. Yes, we were brothers in Christ, but I needed to be known as Boyd. I agree, Boyd is a strange Southern name, normally used as a last name and so somewhat harder to remember, but the patronizing overuse of "brother" certainly bothered me.

My boss's office was not near mine; he led from a position of seclusion, so we seldom saw one another—maybe an occasional all-staff meeting or annual retreat. With so many staff (around 200), and frequent turnover, name recognition required focused attention—attention my boss did not give. Verbalizing a name validates a person's unique creation in Christ.

A Neighbor Who Called Me Wade

We lived briefly in a rental house in our new town while waiting to find a more permanent home to purchase. The neighbor across the street called me Wade from day one. I must have reminded him of a Wade from his past or maybe one in his present. I cordially corrected him to no avail, so I eventually just responded to Wade. Wade is not a bad name—it's just not my name. Because of the brevity of our stay (six months), and the fact that my neighbor couldn't remember the most basic aspect of my identity (my name), I was not surprised that we failed to forge a friendship. Pronouncing a name accurately and spelling it correctly communicates to people that they matter, that you care, and that you want to get to know them.

A Monk Who Called Me Boyd

I met a monk a few years back who looked into my eyes and called me Boyd. "Boyd, nice to meet you." "Boyd, come on back and let's visit." "Boyd, I'm a Michigan State Spartan college football fan." Boyd, Boyd, Boyd—a dozen times he genuinely and affectionately addressed me and looked me in the eyes, with a "yes" on his face that said, "Yes, I want to know you. You are a special child of God, created in His image for good works. You mean something to me because you mean so much to your heavenly Father." He closed our 40-minute time together with this prayer, "Heavenly Father, I pray for my brother Boyd, for You to glorify Yourself through his life and that he would bear much fruit. In Jesus's name, amen." Hearing our name in prayer may be the greatest form of validation and love. Remember others' names and pray for them by name. I only spoke with this monk for 40 minutes, but he marked me with love—for life.

> **TAKEAWAY:** *Relational leaders show affection and affirmation when they speak a person's name.*

Ideas to Help Remember Names

1. Don't say, "I'm bad with names." It may be true for now, but it is self-defeating.

2. When you meet a new friend, say her name back to her and ask what she is excited about. For example: "Pam, nice to meet you. Pam, what are you excited about these days?"

3. The next time you see her and you are not sure of her name, be honest and ask, "It's Pam, right?"

4. Associate a name with something memorable. I met Cecilia at work a couple years ago. I told Cecilia that she reminded me of a 70s song that had her name in it. This kind of association can help you.

5. When on a phone conversation for the first time with someone, write down her name as a reminder and capture any interesting facts about her family, work, or life.

6. When around service staff with name tags or names printed on their uniform, look them in the eyes and thank them by name for a job well done. And give them a nice tip!

7. With uniquely spelled names, ask the person to
   pronounce his name, so you honor him with the correct
   pronunciation.

Names matter because people matter—so look people in their eyes and say their name. And then you will say: you're special, you're important, I care about you, I want to know you better.

> **Point to Ponder:** Learn someone's name and you earn the right to get to know them better.

Relational Leaders Avoid Publicly Shaming Someone

I remember the hurt and shame of being called a slang name in middle school. The Vietnam War was winding down, but two classmates found entertainment by labeling me with a certain Asian slur. Even though I did not know what the three-word description meant, I knew their words were not meant as a compliment. I stuffed my feelings of inferiority and anger—and later vented through the organized violence of the football field. Name calling strips another of dignity and reveals the perpetrator to be ignorant, insecure, and unkind.

> **Point to Ponder:** Avoid the temptation to tear down with name calling, but instead, build up by honoring others' names.

Relational Leaders Are Not Rude

"Love is not rude" (1 Corinthians 13:4-5 NLT), says Paul. Love rejects rudeness because rudeness is the domain of the insensitive and the insecure. Rudeness is impolite and disrespectful. Rude people use coarse words that rub their listeners the wrong way. They are insensitive in the timing and the tone of their conversations. They hurt feelings readily and seem to alienate people on purpose. Love is the light that leads rudeness out of darkness (Romans 2:19).

A rude person is challenging to work alongside because you never know when they are going to offend you or someone else. You lose confidence in rude people because of their volatile nature. You do not want to be embarrassed around one of their outbursts or social indiscretions, so you flee their presence. Rude people become loners by a simple process of elimination of people willing to endure their rudeness. Over time, no one can tolerate their barrage of irreverence and sarcasm. Even the most accepting and forgiving saints grow weary of rudeness. Rudeness has no place in a caring culture.

TAKEAWAY: *Relational leaders love people by cultivating a culture of care.*

Love Expunges Rudeness by Honoring Others

Love expunges rudeness like a healthy body does a virus. Love uses tough love to escort rudeness out the door of relationship. Because you love them and those they influence, you need to be very direct and matter-of-fact in your communication with a rude person. Direct conversation is the only way they begin to "get it." Love takes the time to be very candid and clear with rude people who run roughshod over others. However, be careful not to be rude in dealing with those who are rude. Do not lower your standards to theirs. Be prayerful and filled up with the Spirit before you encounter the rude with truth (Romans 9:1).

Loving people are able to find at least one thing they admire in someone else. Even if a person is full of himself, loving leaders firmly believe that there lies dormant, within him or her, *some* redeeming quality. Love is able to identify the potential for good that lies deep within a selfish soul, just as Barnabas saw potential in Saul (Acts 9:27). Love looks beyond the hard, crusty exterior of someone's character and understands that fear may have locked his or her love away in solitary confinement. Rude people feel lost, lonely, and afraid. Nonetheless, love empowers rude people to grow in faith—faith in God, faith in oneself, and faith in others. Faith frees us from rudeness.

> **Point to Ponder:** *Loving people are able to find at least one thing they admire in someone else.*

The Almighty transforms an impolite heart into one full of kindness and grace. When love has its way, rudeness runs away. Love the rude and watch what God can do! Sarcasm is a smoke screen that hides a lonely, loveless, and hurt heart. Rude people are trying to reach out, but they don't know how. Stay committed to your rude roommate, relative, parent, child, or colleague. Your unconditional love will melt away their iceberg-like insecurities. Pray they will see themselves as Christ sees them, and pray they will love and be loved. Be persistent. Love without condition. Watch the rude person's walls come down as you bombard them with consistent acts of love. Relational leaders love even those who are hard to love.

> **TAKEAWAY:** *By God's grace, relational leaders grow a heart full of kindness and grace.*

Relational Leaders Pray for Others by Name

My friend Gayle called me after his transforming weekend at Promise Keepers. You may recall the men's ministry movement in the mid-1990s calling men to be the husbands and fathers the Lord expected. To my pleasant surprise, Gayle insisted, "Boyd, I want to connect with you by phone every Friday, so I can pray for you. I don't want anything from you, I just want God's best for you and your family." Wow! I felt incredibly encouraged and inspired by a simple, scheduled prayer from a loving friend.

As an associate pastor, I often felt the needs of others pulling on my heart and mind throughout the week. I was glad to give counsel, serve, and speak. But by mid-week, when I began to feel emotional exhaustion, I took solace in the fact that Friday was coming, and with it an unhurried time to connect with my friend. I anticipated those Friday calls with joy; I couldn't wait to be embraced by his kindness and generosity of spirit.

For a year we connected weekly, and Gayle's prayers beautifully connected me to my Savior and Lord Jesus. My friend served me unselfishly with purposeful prayer and encouragement! When we connect people to Christ, they are able to hear from their Creator, who has their best interest in mind. The Lord becomes their chief counselor, and the Holy Spirit their advocate.

Gayle invested in me weekly with an encouraging prayer which produced ongoing dividends of peace, hope, and faith for me and joy, fulfillment, and refreshment for him. Small time investments can produce big returns!

Point to Ponder: Prayer is intimate care for others.

A Powerful Relational Investment in Which Everyone Can Participate

Prayer for one another is a spiritual secret weapon. It rocks the devil's world, wins over a lost world, and brings peace. Prayer for others is a necessary ingredient in the recipe for successful living. A prayer investment is an eternal investment. Prayers for healing, prayers for wisdom, prayers of praise, and prayers to courageously spread the gospel all acknowledge the Lord's priorities. "The prayer offered in faith will make the sick person well; the Lord will raise them up. If they have sinned, they will be forgiven. Therefore confess your sins to each other and pray for each other so that you may be healed. The prayer of a righteous person is powerful and effective" (James 5:15-17). Prayer promotes God's agenda.

Our prayers for others also change us. When we implore Christ to heal the illness of a sweaty-browed small child, our heart grows tender. When we ask God to give a friend wisdom in a crucial decision, we grow in wisdom. When we pray to the Lord of the harvest to send forth laborers, the Spirit directs us to share the good news of Jesus

Christ. Prayer is a platform that produces righteous results for the giver and the receiver.

TAKEAWAY: *Relational leaders pray faith-filled prayers for others during times of crisis.*

Be known as a person who genuinely prays for others, and your network will grow in proportion to the capacity you have to personally pray for others. Relational leaders make themselves known and get to know others. They are vulnerable with their struggles and needs and, at the same time, are interested in others' needs.

Summary of Chapter Six Takeaways

1. Relational leaders show affection and affirmation when they speak a person's name.

2. Relational leaders love people by cultivating a culture of care.

3. By God's grace, relational leaders grow a heart full of kindness and grace.

4. Relational leaders pray faith-filled prayers for others during times of crisis.

Chapter Seven

Be Available and Engaged

*Our presentable parts need no special treatment. But God has put
the body together, giving greater honor to the parts that lacked it,
so that there should be no division in the body, but that its parts
should have equal concern for each other. If one part suffers, every
part suffers with it; if one part is honored, every part rejoices with it.*

1 Corinthians 12:24-26

Jesus Illustrates How to Be Available and Engaged

Jesus tells the story of a generous lover, famously known as the "Good Samaritan." "But a Samaritan, as he traveled, came where the man was; and when he saw him, he took pity on him. He went to him and bandaged his wounds, pouring on oil and wine. Then he put the man on his own donkey, brought him to an inn and took care of him" (Luke 10:33-34). In contrast to the priest and Levite, religious leaders disinterested and too busy to care for the very one they were called to love, he takes the time to care for a fellow human being who has been beaten, robbed, and left for dead. With a twist of irony, Jesus crafts His story with a hero and villains, vividly illustrating the injustice of racism and absurdity of religious hypocrisy. Yes, Samaritans were looked down on as second-class citizens, yet this Samaritan bent down to bind up the wounds of the broken. The professional "do-gooders" were revered, yet they were carried along in their self-absorbed busyness. Jesus reminds us how making ourselves available to help trumps cheap talk. Making ourselves available for service helps us live out faith and love.

Many of us have a lot going on (probably too much). But we never know how a little interest in a restaurant server or a prayer for his future may be a much-needed comfort to draw him to Christ. When someone walks into our office and asks, "Do you have a minute?" that is when we move from around our desk and offer them a chair so we can look face to face with no object between us. Only then are we truly available to engage her heart and feel her pain, help process her confusion or brainstorm ideas. When we look around intently, we will see broken hearts in need, much as the Good Samaritan saw the man in need.

> **TAKEAWAY:** *Relational leaders are generous with their time, and the Lord redeems their time by expanding their capacity to carry out His will.*

Relational Leaders Initiate Screen-Free Conversations

Recently a friend took me to lunch. His agenda was simple—he just wanted to hear how I was doing. What a gift! For more than an hour, Bill just wanted me to talk about what the Lord was teaching me, how my family was doing, and how he could pray for me. His phone was nowhere to be seen or heard, his eye contact was unbroken, and his emotional engagement was energizing. My special friend gave me the gift of his uninterrupted presence. With unhurried interest, I felt loved, understood, valued, and heard. My friend's presence was a gift of love!

Jesus taught compellingly about the importance of truly paying attention and listening to the life lessons found in His teachings. "So pay attention to how you hear. To those who listen to my teaching, more understanding will be given. But for those who are not listening, even what they think they understand will be taken away from them" (Luke 8:18 NLT). Because He illustrated truth with everyday examples, He made it easy for people to understand, but the deepest understanding only came to those who were intellectually, spiritually, physically, and emotionally engaged in hearing what Christ had to say. For believers, being present in the presence of Jesus is not passive prayer, but proactive listening. The heart hears best when it has been cleansed by the Spirit and eagerly communes with Christ.

"I delight in your instructions. My suffering was good for me, for it taught me to pay attention to your decrees. Your instructions are more valuable to me than millions in gold and silver" (Psalm 119:70-72 NLT).

Point to Ponder: Being present to listen to a friend's heart is a generous gift to their emotional well-being.

Who hungers for you to be fully present when you are with them? A spouse, child, friend, or work associate? Being truly present is the fruit of trust. You must trust that other responsibilities can wait, and that by taking a break from obsessing over "critical" issues, you can then reengage, invigorated with new insight. By investing 100% in a conversation with a coworker, you can trust that the Lord is at work in ways all around you—He is moving the hearts of authorities and procuring resources to support your opportunities. By being present, you make a statement of trust that God is at work!

TAKEAWAY: *The Lord may encourage us as relational leaders to rest, recover, and reflect.*

God Is Always Present and Never Leaves Those He Loves

God the Son saves a lost soul once and for all—God the Father comforts and corrects His child—God the Spirit seals a believer with eternal security. There is a completeness that accompanies faith in Christ. He is stable in the middle of instability. He is a rock in the center of swirling circumstances. He is a light that disturbs the darkest darkness. The Lord does not let go of what's His. Once a child of God, always a child of God! "Be strong and courageous. Do not be afraid or terrified because of them, for the LORD your God goes with you; he will never leave you nor forsake you" (Deuteronomy 31:6).

But we may ask, "What about past indiscretions that brought shame and embarrassment?" "Can't foolish living disqualify me from being a Christian?" Eternal salvation and acceptance are not based on our fickle behavior, but on Christ's unchanging character. We can stray, but He is there. We can doubt, but He is there. We can mess up, but He is there. The Lord is always there to lift us up, give us hope, offer us wisdom and fully restore us. We serve with success when we are present in the Lord's presence to hear His voice.

> **Point to Ponder:** God is ever present in our lives to point us to His purposes.

Relational Leaders Are Available and Engaged with God

We do not strive to gain God's acceptance or somehow earn His good graces—peace of mind and a courageous heart come from accepting the fact that you are already accepted by His beloved son Jesus. The idol of money is cruel and causes consternation when your net worth becomes the measure of your worth. "Keep your lives free from the love of money and be content with what you have, because God has said, 'Never will I leave you; never will I forsake you'" (Hebrews 13:5). Lasting security comes from abiding in the faith fortress of your Savior Jesus.

Fear takes a back seat when your faith in Christ drives your life. Like an impatient and immature child yells from the back of the car, "How long before we get there?!" so fear screams doubts and worries about the Lord's timing. As co-pilots with Christ, we must dismiss those distracting voices and look forward by faith. Jesus already has the wheel of your life, so you can confidently trust His will. Have no fear, because He is present to steer you clear of confusion. He never leaves you! As God told Joshua, "No one will be able to stand against you all the days of your life. As I was with Moses, so I will be with you; I will never leave you nor forsake you" (Joshua 1:5).

> **TAKEAWAY:** Relational leaders are available and engaged with God.

By faith, be available and engaged with those the Lord brings into your life every day. Family, friends, acquaintances, and strangers desire and deserve our undivided attention. Generously give the gift of time and trust the Lord to redeem your investment with even more capacity to serve. We can rest in the assurance of Christ's presence.

Summary of Chapter Seven Takeaways

1. Relational leaders are generous with their time, and the Lord redeems their time by expanding their capacity to carry out His will.

2. The Lord may encourage us as relational leaders to rest, recover, and reflect.

3. Relational leaders are available and engaged with God.

Chapter Eight

Seek Wisdom from Scripture

I will delight myself in Your statutes;
I will not forget Your word.

Psalm 119:16 nkjv

Am I learning how to use my Bible? The way to become
complete for the Master's service is to be well soaked in the
Bible: some of us only exploit certain passages. Our Lord
wants to give us continuous instruction out of His Word;
continuous instruction turns hearers into disciples.

Oswald Chambers

Jesus Sought the Scriptures for Wisdom

Jesus not only knew the Scriptures, He also knew the grave error of not knowing the Scriptures. Biblical ignorance results in a life devoid of the power of God. Jesus, full of the Spirit and full of the Word of God, enjoyed the favor of God. "Jesus replied, 'Are you not in error because you do not know the Scriptures or the power of God?'" (Mark 12:24). He did not use Scripture for His own agenda, but followed His Father's instructions. Jesus was the Word who became flesh so that He might model its truth and teach its meaning. During His time on earth, Scripture was the main course of His spiritual diet. Knowing and doing the Word of God qualifies us to instruct and train others in Scripture.

> **Point to Ponder:** Scripture welcomes us to rest in God's power to overcome our problems.

Relational Leaders Have a Spiritual Growth Plan

Scripture memorization is a spiritual growth plan against sin, Satan, and self. It is also God's primary method of conforming us to the image of His Son Jesus Christ. We all are privileged to renew our minds with the truth of Scripture and to cleanse our hearts with the purifying Word of God. "I have hidden your word in my heart that I might not sin against you" (Psalm 119:11).

My hope is that we could commit to memory a verse a week related to what we are experiencing in life. Over the course of a year we will hide 52 nuggets of spiritual nourishment within our soul so that, when needed, the Spirit can bring to mind what has been deposited deep within our hearts.

We may not be the best at memorization, but we do remember what engages our affections. We have the ability to retain sports statistics and other details related to interests or hobbies. Why could we not do this with Scripture too? We need not be intimidated, but to work within our God-given abilities. We should start with a systematic plan to retain the Word of the Lord.

The Lord reveals Himself through His Word (cf. 1 Samuel 3:21). As we increasingly desire to know God, love God, and obey God, His Word makes its way into the crevices of our character. We are being conformed to the character of Christ as we mature in our understanding of the Word made flesh. We grow in our love for the Word as we grow in our love for Jesus, since He was the Word revealed on earth. God's secret weapon of Scripture memorization grows us into the likeness of Christ.

TAKEAWAY: *Relational leaders study Scripture to love God, know God, and obey God.*

We would be wise to see Scripture memory as a blessing, not a burden. Be creative. We can listen to God's Word as we commute to work, exercise, or do chores around the house. Furthermore, we follow Jesus's example when we say to Satan: "It is written." God's Word, written on our hearts through memorization and meditation, equips us to stand strong in Him. The spiritual growth plan of memorizing His Word is used by seasoned saints who deeply know and love the Lord: "How can a young person stay on the path of purity? By living according to your word" (Psalm 119:9).

> **Point to Ponder:** Knowing and obeying Scripture gives us the confidence to invest in others.

A Book Club with Biblical Content

My friend of 25 years, David, and I started a book club five years ago. We invited his son Nathan and Nathan's business partner Mike to join us. Our group still meets once every three weeks to get to know each other and to read and discuss ideas and biblical principles that contribute to successful living. We define successful living as being at peace with God, relationally healthy, financially generous, and intentionally loving others. Our first book was Tony Dungy's biography *Quiet Strength*, and our most recent is Patrick Morley's revised *Man in the Mirror*. The attractiveness of the lives we have studied compels us to model their "best practices" for life. Our lives have changed for the better! I have discovered that focusing on the truth of Scripture with a small group grows us closer to Christ and to each other.

> **TAKEAWAY:** Relational leaders invest in others through small group discussions around biblical principles.

Because of our investment in and love for each other, we have discovered opportunities to do life and business together. We trust each other and understand the strengths and weaknesses we all bring to the table. Recently, one member of our group invited me to serve as a trustee on a significant trust to provide ideas and leadership for the 30-something-year-old who is responsible for using these resources to make the world a better place. This is no insignificant task! Were it not for the friendships built through our close-knit small group, I likely would not have this important opportunity.

Point to Ponder: *We love others like Jesus when we make the Word of God a priority in our learning and our discussions about life.*

A Sample Bible Study Process to Share with Others

When you study Scripture, take care not to be cavalier with the context. Context matters! Study Scripture to grow in humility and grace, so that you can hear Christ calling. Study Scripture not for information and ego's sake, but for instruction, inspiration, and intimacy. Sin can keep you from the Bible or the Bible can keep you from sin. Study to know His story to better define your story!

Below is an outline for developing a regular routine of studying God's Holy Word:

1. Select a Bible Translation: The New International Version is reliable, easy to understand, and accurate. Other helpful versions are the New American Standard (very literal), The Message (written in modern language), and the New King James (it has beautiful verbal images).

2. Choose Commentaries and Study Resources: Scripture study aids are critical in gaining an understanding of the cultural context during Christ's era and the meaning of biblical words and phrases. Paul was a scholar who never stopped learning and relied on books and resources outside of God's Word for his growth and understanding in spiritual matters. He even told Timothy the following: "When you come, bring the cloak that I left with Carpus at Troas, and my scrolls, especially the parchments" (2 Timothy 4:13). Excellent resources are Matthew Henry's Commentary of the Bible (the app is outstanding), Vine's Expository Dictionary (for Greek word studies) and Unger's Bible Dictionary (gives a good cultural understanding).

3. Cross-reference Related Scriptures: The Bible is the best commentary on the Bible. As Paul wrote, "Everything that was written in the past was written to teach us, so that through the endurance taught in the Scriptures and the encouragement they provide we might have hope" (Romans 15:4). Jesus came to fulfill the Law, not to destroy the Law, so ask as you are studying, "What's another verse that might clarify a passage I am seeking to understand and apply?" A great tool for finding cross-references is Biblegateway.com, which lists related verses under the verse you searched for on your screen.

4. Define the Context: Context is critical to understanding the world of those the writings in the Bible were addressing. Understanding the customs, traditions, and mores of ancient cultures brings clarity to what was being said. For example, research into agrarian illustrations and Jewish traditions brings out nuances of occupational and religious details. Cultural familiarity is necessary for an accurate interpretation of the text of Scripture. Furthermore, the type of writing should be taken into consideration. Different kinds of writings (poetry, historical narrative, prophecy, praise, and parables) were used for different purposes.

5. Observe: After you learn the context of the passage and its meaning, read the passage with fresh eyes and an open heart. As Proverbs puts it, "I applied my heart to what I observed and learned a lesson from what I saw" (Proverbs 24:32). Look closely for a pattern or contrast in thinking (that happens a lot in Proverbs). Why are certain details described and others left out? Begin to build a mental bridge from what the Lord was saying then to what He is saying for today.

6. Gain Understanding: Ask the Holy Spirit to show you exactly what He is saying; ask Him for wisdom and

discernment. Your Bible study is a spiritual transaction of truth. His Word is a love letter to you and for you in your time of need. His precepts pulsate with life. As the psalmist says, "I gain understanding from your precepts; therefore I hate every wrong path" (Psalm 119:104).

7. Apply: The Bible is worth a lifetime of study and application. Because we are all in the process of growing in grace, the Holy Spirit is able to teach us at our own pace and perception. He reveals the truth as we are able to live it out with grace and for God's glory.

Below is an example of what this interpretive process might look like when applied to Mark 7:10-12.

> Moses said, "Honor your father and mother," and, "Anyone who curses their father or mother is to be put to death." But you say that if anyone declares that what might have been used to help their father or mother is Corban (that is, devoted to God)—then you no longer let them do anything for their father or mother. (Mark 7:10-12)

a. Select a Bible translation: New International Version.

b. Choose Commentaries and Study Resources:

- Vine's Dictionary definition of "honor" is "to value at a great price, the same word used to honor Christ."

- Matthew Henry Commentary: "Where will men stop, when once they have made the Word of God give way to their tradition? God's statutes shall not only lie forgotten, as antiquated obsolete laws, but they shall, in effect, stand repealed, that their traditions might take place."

- Unger Bible Dictionary offers the following definition of "Corban": "Literally an offering, common to any sacred gift; the term is used to denote sacrifice. All things or persons consecrated for religious purposes become Corban and belong to the sanctuary. The gift giver was relieved from using this gift to God for their parents. This Jesus declared to be contradictory of the command that taught children to honor their parents."

c. Cross-Reference Related Scriptures:

- Mark 7:10—"Honor your father and your mother, so that you may live long in the land the Lord your God is giving you" (Deuteronomy 5:16; see also Exodus 20:12).

- Mark 7:10—"Anyone who curses their father or mother is to be put to death" (Leviticus 20:9; see also Exodus 21:17).

- Mark 7:11—"Those who guide this people mislead them, and those who are guided are led astray" (Isaiah 9:16).

- Mark 7:11—"Make a plate of pure gold. Engrave on it as on a seal: 'Holy to God.' Tie it with a blue cord to the front of the turban. It is to rest there on Aaron's forehead. He'll take on any guilt involved in the sacred offerings that the Israelites consecrate, no matter what they bring. It will always be on Aaron's forehead so that the offerings will be acceptable before God" (Exodus 28:36-38 MSG).

d. Define the Context: Jesus is speaking to powerful religious leaders (the Pharisees) who were jealous of His popularity and who did not like for their authority and teachings to be questioned, much less dismissed. Jesus challenged the most influential religious institution of His day.

e. Observe: Jesus refers to a trusted resource and leader, Moses, whom His audience would respect and consider as valid and reliable. Christ challenges the motivation of public offerings to God that justify the private neglect of a parents' needs.

f. Gain Understanding: Religious pride is a temptation for any of us who are serious about our spiritual walk. We need to make sure Scripture validates our traditions so that our religious assumptions do not void the commands of Christ.

g. Apply: How can I honor God and, at the same time, honor my parents? Perhaps I pray and look for ways to be generous toward the Lord with my time and money, and, at the same time, be generous toward my parents with my time and money.

Conclusion

There are a variety of ways to study the Bible. Find one that fits your style and season in the faith. Though not perfect, this process is one I have used and modified over the years to keep my approach to Scripture sacred, simple, and applicable. Enjoy the journey of growing in your knowledge of Jesus so that you are able to love others how Jesus loves them!

> **TAKEAWAY:** *Relational Leaders embrace a system to study and apply the Scriptures, so they can instruct other hungry hearts in how to do the same.*

Summary of Chapter Eight Takeaways

1. Relational leaders study Scripture to love God, know God, and obey God.

2. Relational leaders invest in others through small group discussions around biblical principles.

3. Relational Leaders embrace a system to study and apply the Scriptures, so they can instruct other hungry hearts in how to do the same.

Chapter Nine

Be a Good Griever

*When Mary reached the place where Jesus was and saw
him, she fell at his feet and said, "Lord, if you had been
here, my brother would not have died." When Jesus saw her
weeping, and the Jews who had come along with her also
weeping, he was deeply moved in spirit and troubled.*

JOHN 11:32-33

*There is a sacredness in tears. They are not the mark of
weakness, but of power. They speak more eloquently than ten
thousand tongues. They are the messengers of overwhelming
grief, of deep contrition, and of unspeakable love.*

WASHINGTON IRVING

Jesus Was a Good Griever

When Jesus saw her weeping, and the Jews who had come along with her also weeping, he was deeply moved in spirit and troubled. "'Where have you laid him?' he asked. 'Come and see, Lord,' they replied. *Jesus wept.* Then the Jews said, 'See how he loved him!' But some of them said, 'Could not he who opened the eyes of the blind man have kept this man from dying?'" (John 11:33-37, emphasis added).

Not long ago, I woke up knowing that I will not see or talk to my mom again in this life. Just past midnight on one night in September of 2018, according to the coroner's report, she was delivered from her intense pain and anguish and she went to be with the Lord. At the funeral home, I wept over her with my two brothers, though I felt God's comfort embrace me in the knowledge that she now had an eternal home where cruel cancer is extinct. My prayer at that time was that

I would be able to love my family well and honor my mom during a time of intense sadness.

In His mercy, the Lord uses life to illustrate His love and grace. The week began with rejoicing in the birth of our granddaughter, Myra Jane, and ended with mourning for my mom. Birth sows tears of joy and thanksgiving, while death harvests tears of grief and gratitude. Birth embraces a created body and soul into a temporal life—death discards a body and escorts a soul into eternal life. Birth begins memories—death ends memories. Birth is Act 1, while death is the curtain call of our life story. There is a tear in every heart, because love cherishes life and death.

Relational Leaders Weep with Those Who Weep

Jesus was one acquainted with grief and given to a good cry. Because He cared much, He cried much. In the gospel passage above, John captures the extremely emotional encounter of Jesus and His friends as they mourn over the death of their friend and brother Lazarus. A man who had recently been full of life was now prematurely dead. Fortunately, Jesus showed up, but to some, His timing should have been sooner so that He could have saved His friend's life. But God's timing is not always our timing, and His plans are for the greater good of His glory. By waiting, Jesus brought to life what had died, instead of healing a life that was already alive. Jesus explained later that belief in God brings glory to God. His power over death deepened His followers' faith in Him as Savior.

> **Point to Ponder:** God's timing is not always our timing, and His plans are for the greater good.

Like Jesus, we can be present and weep with those who are grieving. Tears communicate a tender, uncanny, unspoken language of the heart, mind, and soul. Moist eyes allow us to see and feel our heavenly Father's comfort and love and the comfort and love of His people. I miss my mom; my heart aches and breaks. I want to know her better and I want her to know me better. She does know me better now, and

I will one day know her better when I join her on the other side. My heart can't wait!

I want to share with you the beautiful words of Charles Spurgeon from *Beside Still Waters*:

> Life is like a parade that passes before your eyes. It comes. Hear the people shouting. It is here. In a few minutes, people crowd the streets. Then it vanishes and is gone. Does life strike you as being just that? I remember, ah I remember, so many in the parade. I have stood, as it were, at a window, even though I have also been in the procession. I recall the hearty men of my boyhood, whom I used to hear pray. They are now singing up yonder. I remember a long parade of saints who have passed before me and have gone into glory. What a host of friends we have in the unseen world, which is "gone over to the majority." As we grow older, they are the majority, for our friends on earth are outnumbered by our friends in heaven. Some of you will fondly remember loved ones who have passed away in the parade. But please remember that you are also in the parade. Though they seem to have passed before you, you have been passing along with them, and soon you will reach the vanishing point. We are all walking in the procession.

"Now we who have believed enter that rest, just as God has said" (Hebrews 4:3).

> **TAKEAWAY:** *Relational leaders are acquainted with grief and given to a good cry.*

Relational Leaders Grieve Well

Leaders who lament well grow their capacity to lead well. When a friend or even an enemy falls from this fragile life, a leader who grieves over his loss honors the deceased, as David did: "Then David and all the men with him took hold of their clothes and tore them. They mourned

and wept and fasted till evening for Saul and his son Jonathan, and for
the army of the LORD and for the nation of Israel, because they had
fallen by the sword" (2 Samuel 1:11-12). Dignity and respect resonate
through a life that values another life. The best leaders do not gloat over
an enemy's demise; rather, they see them (with their conflicting values)
as a person created in the image of God. Grief is God's way of helping
us slow down to remember what's most important to Him.

David modeled what it meant to honor someone in death in spite
of their extreme differences. Saul, who out of jealous rage had maneu-
vered to kill David, instead met his own fate. David, who refrained
from attacking the king in his lifetime, did not attack him after his
death. He chose to grieve rather than gloat. David also instructed his
military to stand down and mourn the loss of his friend Jonathan. "I
grieve for you, Jonathan my brother; you were very dear to me. Your
love for me was wonderful, more wonderful than that of women"
(2 Samuel 1:26). Grief preceded any attempt to gain power or affluence.

Leaders must be careful not to rush through lamenting over the
loss of a loved one. Work can wait. Problems can be solved by another.
Invite mourning like you would a wise and compassionate guest over
for dinner conversation. If you fail to feel your sorrow, you will miss
out on the comfort of other Christians and sweet sympathy from the
Man of Sorrows, Jesus. Grief is God's way to draw you closer to Him
and to increase your capacity for empathy. Empty your emotional cup
of anger and fill it with mourning that God can convert to comfort.

Point to Ponder: Grief is God's way to draw us closer to Him
and to enlarge our empathy.

Jesus was acquainted with grief. He wept. He mourned. He ago-
nized over the loss of sweet fellowship with His Father. He embraced
friends and cried over the death of a friend. The comfort of Christ is
necessary for a Christian's heart to be infused with divine comfort,
to be healed and equipped to comfort others. Beware of the temptation to be "self-reliant," to avoid being a "burden" on others. Burdens
become blessings when others support you in your loss. A leader with

true humility exposes her grieving heart to God's grace and love. As David wrote, "Listen to my words, LORD, consider *my lament*. Hear my cry for help, my King and my God, for to you I pray. In the morning, LORD, you hear my voice; in the morning I lay my requests before you and wait expectantly" (Psalm 5:1-3, emphasis added). Cry. Mourn. Be raw. Be sad. Be sorry for your loss. Be comforted. Learn to grieve well. Lament.

> **TAKEAWAY:** *When experiencing sorrow, relational leaders go to the Man of Sorrows, Jesus.*

Relational Leaders Grieve, Receive Comfort, and Give Comfort

"Praise be to the God and Father of our Lord Jesus Christ, the Father of compassion and the God of all comfort, who comforts us in all our troubles, so that we can comfort those in any trouble with the comfort we ourselves receive from God" (2 Corinthians 1:3-4). What sorrows lie deep on the bottom of the sea of your soul? What sorrows have you suppressed that cry out for comfort and grieving? Maybe abuse has robbed you of your dignity or the wound of a severed relationship still festers in anger and bitterness. Like a bad dream, you may relive a life-altering experience you have never truly mourned and received the healing comfort and love of others. Like learning a new language, you may stumble with words to express your emotions, so let your tears do the talking. Bare your soul in a safe environment of other caring souls so they can care for you and comfort you. Dredge up sorrows deep in your soul, grieve them and be comforted, and you will grow your capacity to comfort others. God comforts you in all troubles.

> **Point to Ponder:** *A soul ravaged by sorrow cannot heal itself without the comfort of love and kindness.*

Cry out to Christ, for He cries with you. He is your joy in life and your comforter in death. Jesus is your hope in your sickness and your strength in your sorrows. The Lord is your peace in the storm and your living water during your spiritual drought. God is your fortress of faith as you battle your fears and a refuge of acceptance when you suffer rejection. Christ perfects His love in you through grief. As John writes, "If we love one another God remains in us and His love is brought to perfection in us" (1 John 4:12 NAB). Mourn, be blessed, and be comforted. God loves you.

TAKEAWAY: *Relational leaders who mourn well are comforted well.*

The Saddest Day of My Life

My mother's memorial service in the fall of 2018 was the saddest day of my life. The reality of my mom's love began to settle in and stretch my soul. Her love is unique, never to be replaced fully by any human substitute. My mom was a single parent, so her love was even weightier as she carried an expanded capacity to fill the void of a father. So I wept and mourned over my mother. My tears were a tribute to her love, how she raised me in an honorable way.

Thankfully, I did not weep alone, as teary hugs from friends and family dampened my cheeks and shoulders. Love and grief weep together to bring comfort and peace. Comforted sorrow expands my capacity to care.

Life consists of losses. The loss of a child. Opportunity loss. Financial loss. Relational loss. Physical loss. Every day we lose a day of life. But one of the most significant is the loss of someone who is dearly loved. When Momma died, a part of me died. A mother's love cannot be replaced. The one whose body I came out of lies horizontal six feet in the earth never to verbally communicate to me her care again. Momma is gone. Her death was the saddest day of my life.

Her battle with ugly cancer was over. Lifeless, only lingering memories hovered over her head, a slight smile, relieved, restful. My brothers, my stepfather, and I wept next to her cold corpse on hold at the funeral home, awaiting in line (#5 on the waiting list, icky) a mournful parade to the crematory.

And what accompanied her departure? Her smile. Her words laced with love, "I'm proud of you, son," and often expressed with keen insight wrapped with worry, "You look tired, you are working too much." Her cooking—she knew how to make food better than it was ever intended to taste. That's what mommas do, especially a mom with sons. Most significantly, love left with her, and perhaps, just perhaps, a single mom necessarily has a double capacity to love for two roles. It hurts…Momma's gone. There is a tear in every heart waiting for comfort to soothe.

I wish I could call Momma. Our every other day phone call doesn't seem frequent enough now. Perhaps I should have called daily, and not be weary of her warnings about the weather and her complaints about her health. Ashamedly, I remember skeptically listening to what was to be her last self-diagnosis of severe abdominal pain—which turned out to be a body ravaged with cancer in the stomach area. A son cannot call his mom too many times. A five-minute chat with Momma was the highlight of her day and a reminder of who raised me. Momma deserved my listening ear.

Life is busy, but what matters most before we bury our parents? Working extra hours, making more money for some uncertain day of maybe having more time at our disposal or taking a day off and hanging out with the one who brought us into this world and who prepared us to live life to the fullest? What would I do different…if I had known 12 months ago Mom would be gone in a year?

I would walk with her a dozen more times around her garden and hear how too much or too little rain is affecting the tomatoes, since nobody romanced homegrown tomatoes like Momma. I would sit on the back porch with her, sip strong dark coffee, and listen to Momma's latest schemes to keep the deer out of her vegetables. I would brush off her three-legged dog Dango a few more aggravating times and send him away with disgust at his smell and deformity. I know I should have more compassion and regard for animals, Momma was working on me, because she sure loved her dogs and cats.

Momma's gone, but the memories of her influence remain alive and well, like a rugged kitchen table beautifully stained and naturally scarred by boiling pots, food spills or permanent moisture rings from water glasses, she will forever mark my life with her words, wisdom, and hard work. I tie a bow on Momma's memory with this tribute only a Southern momma could portray:

MY MOMMA RAISED ME

My momma raised me to:
clean my plate.
That's how my momma raised me!

My momma raised me to:
gargle with Listerine, floss, brush my teeth,
and kiss girls who do the same.
That's how my momma raised me!

My momma raised me to:
wash my hands before dinner—which was lunch,
and before supper—which was dinner.
That's how my momma raised me!

My momma raised me to:
feed the animals or not have any.
That's how my momma raised me!

My momma raised me to:
say yes mam, no mam, thank you mam, please.
That's how my momma raised me!

My momma raised me to:
shoot a squirrel with a .22,
a quail with a .410,
a rabbit with a 16 gauge,
a dove with a 12 gauge,
and a deer with a 30/30.
That's how my momma raised me!

My momma raised me to:

walk bare footed,
carry a cane pole,
dig up red worms,
wet a hook,
catch a fish,
scale 'em, gut 'em, fry 'em up and eat 'em.
That's how my momma raised me!

My momma raised me to:
gig bullfrogs at night
with a spot light,
fry up their legs,
and watch 'em jump around in the pan.
That's how my momma raised me!

My momma raised me to:
catch fire flies, display them in
a quart Mason jar and nail holes in
the tin lid with an eight penny nail.
That's how my momma raised me!

My momma raised me to:
skip rocks on a small pond,
and dream big dreams.
That's how my momma raised me!

My momma raised me to:
eat homemade buttermilk biscuits,
with real butter, sorghum syrup and sweet milk
homemade cornbread cooked in a cast iron black skillet,
fried potatoes, covered with catsup,
fried okra, fried chicken, fried livers and onions,
black eyed peas, field peas, crowder peas and English peas,
pinto beans, green beans, baked beans and white beans.
That's how my momma raised me!

My momma raised me to:
pick blackberries, blueberries and plums.
To bust open a yellow meat watermelon in the field,

suck up the juice, and spit out the slippery black seeds
and to kill snakes in the creek with a hoe.
That's how my momma raised me!

My momma raised me to:
cut down our Christmas tree on her grandmother's land,
somehow tie it on the back and top of our yellow Volkswagen,
and display it proudly in our home, like it was unveiled at
Rockefeller Center in New York City.
That's how my momma raised me!

My momma raised me to:
work hard, tell the truth and be kind to everyone.
That's how my momma raised me!

My momma raised me to:
be polite, be grateful and be compassionate.
That's how my momma raised me!

My momma raised me to:
look people in the eye
and greet 'em with
hello, howdy, good morning,
good afternoon or how you doing?
That's how my momma raised me!

My momma raised me to:
say a blessing before a meal,
enjoy my food or at least act like I did,
take my dishes to the sink and wash 'em.
That's how my momma raised me!

My momma raised me to:
sweep and mop the floor, and vacuum the carpet.
Make my bed, wash my clothes, rake the leaves,
*   mow the grass.*
Pick up pecans and shell 'em.
That's how my momma raised me!

My momma raised me to:

dab alcohol, methylate or mercurochrome on a cut.
That's how my momma raised me!

My momma raised me to:
believe castor oil and duct tape
solved most ailments and fixed broken things.
That's how my momma raised me!

My momma raised me to:
Play sports. Play my best. Play fair.
Play for fun. Play when I was hurt.
Play to help my teammates,
and play to win.
That's how my momma raised me!

My momma raised me to:
read, be curious and ask questions.
Go to college, go to graduate school,
and never stop learning.
That's how my momma raised me!

My momma raised me to:
travel, learn from other cultures and serve people.
That's how my momma raised me!

My momma raised me to:
love all people as individuals made in God's image,
all races, all religions, all political persuasions.
That's how my momma raised me!

My momma raised me to:
drive a stick shift,
change the oil,
wash the outside,
and vacuum out the inside.
That's how my momma raised me!

My momma raised me to:
believe sweat is good, and debt is bad.
That's how my momma raised me!

My momma raised me to:
cry, and to be willing to die, for someone I love.
That's how my momma raised me!

My momma raised me to:
believe comfort relates to proximity,
so when I found her daddy dead,
as a 12-year-old boy,
she let me sleep on the floor
next to her bed for a week.
That's how my momma raised me!

My momma raised me to:
date girls from the south.
That's how my momma raised me!

My momma raised me to:
love the Lord,
and to marry someone
who loved the Lord more than me.
That's how my momma raised me!

My momma raised me to:
read the Bible and do what it says.
That's how my momma raised me!

My momma raised me to:
be my very best.
To be the best Christian.
To be the best coworker.
To be the best friend.
To be the best husband, dad, granddad, and father-in-law.
To be the best son-in-law.
To be the best brother, cousin and grandson.
To be the best son.

Momma this is how you raised me!

You done good momma, you done good.

No more pain, no more worries mom.
Enjoy your rest, and your gardening,

I'll see you soon. I love you.

Summary of Chapter Nine Takeaways

1. Relational leaders are acquainted with grief and given to a good cry.
2. When experiencing sorrow, relational leaders go to the Man of Sorrows, Jesus.
3. Relational leaders who mourn well are comforted well.

Chapter Ten

Comfort Those Who Suffer and Hurt

Praise be to the God and Father of our Lord Jesus Christ,
the Father of compassion and the God of all comfort, who
comforts us in all our troubles, so that we can comfort
those in any trouble with the comfort we ourselves receive
from God. For just as we share abundantly in the sufferings
of Christ, so also our comfort abounds through Christ.

2 CORINTHIANS 1:3-5

She knew the soothing power of a human touch on aching
flesh. Knew the strange bond that formed when two creatures
united in mutual need, one hurting, the other healing.

SUSAN WIGGS, *AT THE KING'S COMMAND*

Jesus Comforted Others

Jesus offers up an incredible truth in His second teaching in the beatitudes. His first teaching defines humility as foundational to coming alive as a citizen in the kingdom of heaven. Next, Jesus instructs us to process our grief so we can be comforted. "Blessed are those who mourn, for they will be comforted" (Matthew 5:4). Sorrow is an everyday occurrence in this world, requiring a comfort that originates in Christ and is lived out by fellow followers of Jesus. The comfort of Christ through other Christians gives us permission to process our grief freely. Like a soldier who is riddled with wounds and incapacitated requires the care of others, so a soul ravaged by sorrow cannot heal itself without the comfort of love and kindness. The Gospel of John gives an example of the power of supporting others in their grief. "And many Jews had come to Martha and Mary to comfort them in the loss of their brother" (John 11:19). If we resort to self-reliance or denial, we miss the therapeutic effects of grieving and remain in discomfort.

Have you lost someone or something close to your heart—a baby, a spouse, a friend, a job, or an opportunity? Great loss requires great grace, and the pain can be unbearable. Loss raises hard questions: Why do some expecting mothers have a stillborn child and others don't? Where is God when emotions are raw and a great hurt settles in the heart? We cannot truly understand these puzzling matters until we get to heaven and are able to ask, "Why, Lord, why?" We don't always understand the ways of God, but we can always count on Christ's comfort. The Lord lingers long with those caught in the pain of great loss. What others cannot totally understand, our heavenly Father fully comprehends. God's grace soothes aching hearts. Christ's comfort is like cool cough syrup flowing down a swollen, inflamed throat. "For just as we share abundantly in the sufferings of Christ, so also our comfort abounds through Christ" (2 Corinthians 1:5).

> **Point to Ponder:** The Lord has a limitless capacity to comfort and cure.

Relational Leaders Are Comforted by Christ So They Can Comfort Others

Furthermore, Christ comforts us so that we are able to extend His comfort to others. Giving comfort is a critical part of God's economy, and those of us saved by grace must not be stingy with its application. Who do you know that needs a listening ear, a silent prayer, or a caring visit?

If we allow our busyness to prevent the sharing of comfort with those in need, then we miss out on one of life's great joys. Tears often lurk under the surface of a tender heart. Look around in your circle of influence—who is struggling with health, work, or relational issues? Seek them out and comfort them. Say a prayer for someone in despair; send flowers to a young mom who just lost her little one after the first trimester of pregnancy, do some networking for an acquaintance in a career transition, pay the rent for a struggling relative, or introduce someone who is broken to the uplifting love and saving power of Jesus Christ. Administering comfort to those who need it is a platform to proclaim God's grace. As Paul wrote, "Praise be to the God and Father of our Lord Jesus Christ, the Father of compassion and the God of all comfort, who comforts us in all our troubles, so that we can comfort those in any trouble with the comfort we ourselves receive from God" (2 Corinthians 1:3-4).

> **TAKEAWAY:** *Relational leaders are comforted by Christ so they can comfort others.*

Giving Permission to Die

"Son if you were me, would you take the chemo?" My momma put the question to me after a sobering visit to her oncologist the day before. Guardedly, I replied, "I don't know." Having anticipated she might ask my advice, I went on. "If I knew I would have five or six months more of quality living I would, but if it means only another month of misery I would not." Then I wept. And only as a mother can, she comforted me. Three days later she decided not to take the chemotherapy, and she died in her sleep. She had granted herself permission to die, and she was soon escorted into eternal love.

> *Point to Ponder: Jesus breathed His last on our behalf!*

Jesus faced death with courage: "Jesus called out with a loud voice, 'Father, into your hands I commit my spirit.' When he had said this, he breathed his last" (Luke 23:46). With the finality of knowing He had finished the works of providing salvation for all who believe and glorifying His heavenly Father on earth, He voluntarily declared, "It is finished." He committed His spirit to the One who gives life to our spirit. With permission from heaven to go back to heaven, Jesus was escorted by 10,000 angels into glory. Eternal love had entered earth, so He could love His creation first-hand. As recipients of His love, we are to go and do likewise until we breathe our last. Jesus breathed His last on our behalf!

Relational Leaders Recognize Death as a Passageway to New Beginnings

Is there someone or something to which you need to give permission to die? A friend or family member who has been lingering may need for you to let go of them in love. Release them from their pain and suffering to go be with their Savior Jesus. Or, you might need to let go of a relationship until new life can be breathed back into it. Death can be a passage to new beginnings. Permission to die leads to life.

Perhaps you have experienced the death of a vision, but your stubborn spirit still clings to its corpse. The Holy Spirit is the incubator of God-given visions, so learn from your last endeavor and lean into the eternal love of your Lord. Let Him birth a new vision in your heart. You might grieve over a stillborn vision, but you must continue to look into the face of Jesus—your ultimate vision. Give permission to die to whatever in your life teeters on the verge of death, so that all might experience new life.

Heavenly Father, give me courage and love to let go of something or someone who lingers on the verge of death. In Jesus's name, amen.

> **TAKEAWAY:** *Relational leaders recognize death as a passageway to new beginnings.*

Missing Mom

My first Thanksgiving without my momma—an indescribable void, my heart longs just to hear her voice, "Yes, son, it would help for you to pick up a ham, and I will have your favorites: a cheese ball with chip beef and scallions, 'doo-dads' [an addictive snack of Chex mix, pretzels, pecans, and peanuts, baked to a crisp and lightly seasoned] and wedding cookies." No longer am I able to enjoy Mom's favorite things that grew into my favorite things. But her caring voice still rings in my heart, "Be careful, son, you need to rest, tell the girls hi, I love you." Momma, I miss you—but I will not forget you. Beyond the grave, your words help me carry on. I love you.

> **Point to Ponder:** *A person who dies with a faith desperate for God is a comfort to those who will one day face death.*

Abel was the one son who brought delight to God by what he brought to God—an acceptable sacrifice. "And Abel also brought an offering—fat portions from some of the firstborn of his flock. The LORD looked with favor on Abel and his offering, but on Cain and his offering he did not look with favor. So Cain was very angry, and his face was downcast" (Genesis 4:4-5). Though dead, Abel still speaks to the living by reminding us to bring to our Savior and Lord all we have with a heart of love and gratitude, as the writer of Hebrews relates: "By faith Abel still speaks, even though he is dead" (Hebrews 11:4). Though the youngest, Abel was able by the grace of God to go directly to God—for every child can equally worship his heavenly Father in Spirit and in truth. Cain was the oldest in age, but he lacked the old soul of his brother who rested in the Lord rather than striving in his own strength to gain divine acceptance. A person who dies with a faith desperate for God is a person whose faith communicates to future generations.

"Firsts" without someone who has died are really hard—first Thanksgiving, first Christmas, first New Year, first Mother's Day, first Father's Day, first birthday, first anniversary, first vacation. Are you experiencing a "first" without someone you love? You pick up the phone to call her, but she is unavailable to answer. You play over a conversation in your mind, but her ears are deaf to your words. You face a stressful situation and you want to process with her, feel her patient presence, hear her wise words—but her personalized ideas and calming tone are not available. If you are alone, I'm so sorry for your loss—my heart hurts for you and with you.

There are many ways to process pain. Perhaps you do so by honoring the one who is gone. Take turns around your holiday dinner table and relive sweet memories. Tell stories full of joy and laughter. Memorialize the traits you remember that influenced you and still make their mark on your life. Celebrate a life by telling how that person brought life to you and your family, whether through stories, quirks, wisdom, love, generosity, prayers, or their listening ear. Honor the life that was by looking for ways to celebrate that life. Though dead, that person can speak, in a manner, through our remembrances of them—so we listen and share stories together.

> *Heavenly Father, I miss my loved one and I lean into*
> *You for comfort and strength. In Jesus's name, amen.*

TAKEAWAY: *Relational leaders honor those who have gone before them in faithfulness and love.*

Relational Leaders Have Faith and Patience to Suffer Well

"Widespread carcinomatosis" was a life-altering prognosis for my mom. We wept. To suffer cancer is a big burden to bear. To see a loved one suffer is a pain that takes faith and patience to process in prayer. It is harrowing to witness a parent once full of life and laughter suddenly ravaged by an incurable disease. It is the same with a child born with an ailment that requires a lifetime of intense medical attention. Most of us will experience the afflictions of someone precious to us who will need us to be strong in their time of need. We suffer with them for their comfort and peace. By God's grace, all are able to suffer well.

Point to Ponder: Walk with others through their valley so they are not alone and remind them of God's river of love that flows through the valley of the shadow of death.

Job, one of God's giants in the faith, found a way to suffer well. Though not always a perfect example of how to handle pain, this man of God experienced deeper faith and patience as he processed his pain out loud to his long-suffering heavenly Father and to his well-meaning, but sometimes impatient, friends. The outcome of the Lord's blessings were not evident to all until *after* Job had endured. As James writes, "Indeed we count them blessed who endure. You have heard of the perseverance of Job and seen the end intended by the Lord—that the Lord is very compassionate and merciful" (James 5:11 NKJV). Christ's compassion and mercy may seem late in coming when we labor under painful conditions, but grace and mercy meet us at the intersection of fear, faith, pain, and perseverance.

Is your heart broken because of the brokenness you see and feel in someone you love? You might second-guess yourself for not doing more, but don't—even if you could have done more, you can't go back and undo the past. Instead, lean into the compassion and mercy of Christ to forgive you, free you, and give you the confidence to stand firm for a friend or family member who has fallen. Walk with her through her valley so that she knows she is not alone. Remind her of God's river of love that flows through the valley of the shadow of death. Allow suffering to stretch your faith to places you've never been so that you can support the frail and the fearful. "Let us then approach the throne of grace with confidence, so that we may receive mercy and find grace to help us in our time of need" (Hebrews 4:16).

You may not know the end that God intends until after you have endured. Keep the wick of your life burning bright for the Lord through rest, soul-care, and earnest prayers from your caring community. As Paul writes, "For just as we share abundantly in the sufferings of Christ, so also our comfort abounds through Christ" (2 Corinthians 1:5). Just as a burning candle lights another candle with nothing lost, so your unwavering faith and patient love ignite the light of comfort, hope, and peace to help another suffer well. Faith and patience to suffer well are drawn from the deep well of knowing God. Live a life story of suffering well, and your faith will instruct and inspire another to suffer well.

> *Heavenly Father, I come to Your throne of grace for*
> *Your great comfort and mercy. In Jesus's name, amen.*

TAKEAWAY: *Relational leaders have the faith and patience to suffer well.*

Summary of Chapter Ten Takeaways

1. Relational leaders are comforted by Christ so they can comfort others.

2. Relational leaders recognize death as a passageway to new beginnings.

3. Relational leaders honor those who have gone before them in faithfulness and love.

4. Relational leaders have the faith and patience to suffer well.

Chapter Eleven

Make Others Successful

*Very truly I tell you, whoever believes in me will do the
works I have been doing, and they will do even greater
things than these, because I am going to the Father.*

JOHN 14:12

*A leader's job is not to do the work for others, it's to help
others figure out how to do it themselves, to get things
done, and to succeed beyond what they thought possible.*

SIMON SINEK

Jesus Makes Others Successful

Jesus expects His followers to see greater things occur than they have
already experienced (see John 1:50). Greater things could be children
who surpass their parents by influencing the world with the gospel.
Greater access to the world may come through building orphanages,
hospitals, and schools in Jesus's name. Think big!

Our salvation is just the beginning of seeing things from the Lord's
perspective. Not only has Christ saved us *from* sin, hell, and self, He has
saved us *for* righteousness, heaven, and Himself. We are not meant to
stay stuck in the initial stages of our conversion, but rather are meant
to move forward, following the Holy Spirit's plan. Our faith experience may surpass those who have influenced our spiritual journey. The
student sometimes sees greater things than the teacher. As Jesus said,
"Very truly I tell you, whoever believes in me will do the works I have
been doing, and they will do even greater things than these, because I
am going to the Father" (John 14:12).

Relational Leaders Make Relational Investments for the Success of Others

Wise individuals do not spend all their income. They have a process. They give and save and do not consume all their cash on themselves. Relationships are like money—we can spend all our efforts seeking what others can do for us, or we can intentionally invest in their lives in ways that make them feel valued and appreciated. Like Paul says, "Remember this: Whoever sows sparingly will also reap sparingly, and whoever sows generously will also reap generously" (2 Corinthians 9:6). Investment in others brings them joy, and the person making the investment receives the palpable dividends: encouragement, hope, and reliable resources.

> **Point to Ponder:** Relationships are like money—we can spend all our efforts seeking what others can do for us, or we can intentionally invest in their lives.

Paul describes the principle of sowing and reaping. Though he applies this process to generosity with money, the same is true of relationships. Paul's audience, who would have been familiar with an agrarian culture, understood that when the soil was prepared and seed was sown in abundance and carefully cultivated, an abundant harvest was soon to come. Generous reaping is the outcome of generous sowing. When we sow love, patience, kindness, and generosity into a relationship, we receive a harvest of the same abundant fruit of the Spirit. As Paul says, "Let us not become weary in doing good, for at the proper time we will reap a harvest if we do not give up" (Galatians 6:9).

What if we approached relationships seeking to give instead of to get? Seek out someone who may be younger but is hungry to grow as a person and follow hard after God's heart. Schedule a monthly meeting to discuss their needs: discerning God's will, overcoming fear, or learning how to become a mature disciple of Christ. Also, share ideas you have about wise money management, an effective prayer life, and how to work with difficult people, to name a few. After your time, enjoy a meal together and discuss heart issues.

Relational investment in others must flow from your relational investment with your heavenly Father. Sow prayer and you will reap a heart of faith. Sow Bible study and you will reap a heart of obedience. Sow praise and worship and you will reap a heart of hope. Invest time with Christ first. This will enable you to invest more greatly in others. Relational investments are your greatest asset, so continue to prosper in true riches. As Paul says, "In this way they will lay up treasure for themselves as a firm foundation for the coming age, so that they may take hold of the life that is truly life" (1 Timothy 6:19).

TAKEAWAY: *Relational leaders invest in others out of the returns on their relational investment with their heavenly Father.*

Relational Leaders Mentor Younger Leaders for Them to Enjoy Success

"At the window of my house I looked out through the lattice. I saw among the simple, I noticed among the young men, a youth who lacked judgment" (Proverbs 7:6-7). Most young people yearn for someone to invest time and wisdom in them. They know deep in their heart that they need help handling their heartaches. They have yet to graduate from the "school of hard knocks," and they need wise and loving instruction. Who in your circle of influence is a candidate for your caring attention? It may be a son or daughter, a colleague at work, or a friend from church. God places people in our lives for a purpose. Perhaps you prayerfully pursue a mentoring relationship with a teachable young person. They can learn from your mistakes as much as, or even more than, they can from your wise choices.

Point to Ponder: Mentors are not perfect, just wiser because of their failures and successes.

Mentors are not perfect, just wiser because of their failures and successes. Look around and ask the Lord to lead you to a young person who may be heading in the wrong direction. Reach out and you will have returned the favor to someone who loved you. Mentors take time for others because they are eternally grateful for those who took time for them. Gratitude to God is a great reason to go the extra mile with someone younger. This kind of mentorship doesn't have to be complicated. One idea is simply to read books together, perhaps a book a month for a year. Meet over coffee to discuss how the book challenged your thinking or changed your behavior for the better.

A young leader can avoid certain problems when she is able to model the wise habits of her mentor. Always invite an older adult into your life who can educate you in the ways of God. Paul says, "Encourage the young women to love their husbands, to love their children...likewise urge the young men to be sensible" (Titus 2:4, 6 NASB). The mentoring process is valuable to both parties. It provides accountability, encouragement, love, and obedience to Christ's commands. Mentor young people so that they will follow the right path and, perhaps, help someone else do the same.

> **TAKEAWAY:** *Relational leaders mentor young leaders so that they will follow the right path and, perhaps, help someone else do the same.*

Relational Leaders Follow a Proven Mentoring Process

Timothy was a protégé of Paul's, but most importantly, he was a follower of Jesus Christ. This young man had a fine spiritual pedigree that he acquired from the sincere faith of his mother and grandmother (see 2 Timothy 1:5). However, as a man just getting started in life, he lacked experience and spiritual maturity. Paul took the time to instruct and inspire Timothy in the ways of the Lord. He mentored him so he could mentor others; as Paul writes, "And the things you have heard me say in the presence of many witnesses entrust to reliable people who will also be qualified to teach others" (2 Timothy 2:2). Mentoring is meant to become a way of life. Intentional investment in leaders helps to grow leaders for Christ.

Point to Ponder: *Mentoring is meant to become a way of life.*

The Lord called my friend Regi to help facilitate a mentoring move-ment called the Radical Mentoring process. I have utilized this nine-month strategy over the years with groups of eight to ten men. I value the experience because it is modeled after the way Jesus interacted with those closest to Him. The once-a-month, three-hour timeframe together provides community, accountability, Scripture memorization, book reports, and prayer. Most of all, we all grew closer to Christ and each other. Today, I have good friends as a result of our walk through this relational and spiritual engagement. "In the same way that iron sharpens iron, a person sharpens the character of his friend" (Proverbs 27:17 THE VOICE).

What does mentorship look like in your life? You know you need a mentor if you are breathing. Look for leaders further down the road in life whom you respect in their roles as dads and moms, husbands and wives. Pray for a role model who is successful at work and home. Their character should be consistent, whether they interact with those who know them the best or those who know them the least. Be prayer-ful and intentional. A mentor may come to you, but make sure to seek someone else to mentor as well.

Make time to become better. Aspire to become like a leader who lives like Jesus Christ.

The healthiest people are mentored by others so that they can men-tor others. As the psalmist writes, "One generation after another will celebrate Your great works; they will pass on the story of Your power-ful acts to their children" (Psalm 145:4 THE VOICE). Mentorship is a lifetime process of receiving and giving. We are the most accountable when, by God's grace, we seek to model what we ask others to do. Men-tors are imperfect, but they follow their perfect Savior and Lord, Jesus. Be vulnerable with your own struggles and sins so that those around you feel free to do the same. Mentoring is not as much a rigid discipline as it is an exercise in meshing our hearts around the heart of our heav-enly Father. "Radical" mentoring is actually the normal Christian life.

TAKEAWAY: *Relational leaders are vulnerable about their own struggles so that those around them feel free to do the same.*

Relational Leaders Invest Relationally Close to Home

"Be sure you know the condition of your flocks, give careful attention to your herds" (Proverbs 27:23). These words remind us that we must attend to the state of our own home and family, our "flock." In that spirit, I recognize my four sons-in-law as some of my most valuable investments. After all, their wives, my daughters, represent my four "pearls of great price." We have regular phone calls, meet in person, and take trips together. I am so proud of these guys for their intentionality in their relationships with God, family, and their work. Though I realize this might sound a bit morbid, I believe we are all seeking to invest in those who will attend our funerals. Our prayer is for those who know us the best to love us the most!

What is a robust relationship? It is healthy, strong, and dependable, and it grows with time. Just like money in an interest-bearing account grows in value over years, so do relationships that are given focused attention. Outside of our time with the Lord, investment in people is our greatest asset.

Point to Ponder: Outside of our time with the Lord, investment in people is our greatest asset.

How do you view your most significant relationships? Your spouse? Your children? Your parents, grandparents, and siblings? Do they feel honored or tolerated by your behavior? Are you proactive or reactive in how you reach out to them? It's even more necessary to initiate relationships with those who are socially immature and who have never had good relational models from which to learn. Those of us who know better are responsible to love on those who don't. As Paul writes, "Don't look out only for your own interests, but take an interest in others, too" (Philippians 2:4 NLT). Relationships require a leader who loves well.

Our relationship with the Lord provides the spiritual stamina and emotional energy to engage others in a meaningful way. To give generously, we have to regularly receive from the One who has bountiful grace and infinite wisdom. Jesus Christ is our relational engineer who, like a gifted architect, is able to build a beautiful bond between those who love, respect, and serve each other. God gives relational freedom. "You, my brothers and sisters, were called to be free. But do not use your freedom to indulge the flesh; rather, serve one another humbly in love" (Galatians 5:13).

TAKEAWAY: *Relational leaders invest in the next generation.*

Summary of Chapter Eleven Takeaways

1. Relational leaders invest in others out of the returns on their relational investment with their heavenly Father.

2. Relational leaders mentor young leaders so that they will follow the right path and, perhaps, help someone else do the same.

3. Relational leaders are vulnerable about their own struggles so that those around them feel free to do the same.

4. Relational leaders invest in the next generation.

Chapter Twelve

Have an Unchanging Identity

He saw the Spirit of God descending like a dove and alighting
upon Him. And suddenly a voice came from heaven, saying,
"This is My beloved Son, in whom I am well pleased."

MATTHEW 3:16-17

The greatest trap in life is not success, popularity, or
power, but self-rejection, doubting who we truly are.

HENRI NOUWEN

Jesus the Unchanging One

Change can be exhausting, or it can be exhilarating. It can blow in my face like a strong nor'easter or be a positive force at my back, pushing me forward with accelerated momentum. In my mind, I like the good change of progress at work, travel, and adventure, but I avoid the bad change of relational conflict and painful health ailments. I am attracted to change I can control, but I am reluctant to embrace change outside of my control.

Thankfully, our Lord and Savior Jesus Christ is unchanging. As the author of Hebrews writes, "Jesus Christ is the same yesterday and today and forever" (Hebrews 13:8). His righteousness is reliable. Christ's character is consistent. Like a loyal lighthouse beckons from the seashore seeking ships lost in a storm or anxious nighttime navigation, our loyal Lord is always available to light our path. Jesus shines the brightest during our darkest days. His unchanging ways give us peace along the way of our ever-changing circumstances. Jesus is dependable when others become undependable. "My God is my rock, in whom I take refuge, my shield and the horn of my salvation. He is my stronghold, my refuge and my savior" (2 Samuel 22:3).

Relational Leaders Walk in Love as Dearly Loved Children of God

When I look in the face of an infant grandchild, I see the influence of several individuals with different last names over successive generations. The eyes of the mom, the forehead of the dad, the cheeks of the grandfather, and the lips of the grandmother. Without understanding who or what brought her into the world, the precious baby already has an identity that will mark her the rest of her life. Just as physical identity is defined by traits passed on by the parents, so our true core identity is defined by the image of God: the Father's wisdom, the Spirit's strength, the Son's love. Our unchanging identity in Christ defines what we do, what we have, how we feel, and what others think.

> *Point to Ponder:* Who we are in Christ is defined by God's image in us and His influence on us. We live attractive lives when our life is defined by our loving Lord.

Paul describes followers of Jesus as dearly loved children who are to walk in the way of love, just as Christ loved us and gave Himself up for us: "Follow God's example, therefore, as dearly loved children and walk in the way of love, just as Christ loved us and gave himself up for us as a fragrant offering and sacrifice to God" (Ephesians 5:1-2). "Dearly loved" to "walk in the way of love"—wow! What freedom to be who God made us to be: loved dearly by our Father in heaven, so we can love others on earth with His same selfless love. Like a beloved child of caring parents, we follow God's example in how we treat others. Who we are in Christ is defined by God's image in us and His influence on us. We live attractive lives when our life is defined by our loving Lord.

Relational Leaders Are Defined by Their Relationship with God

You are free to be who God made you to be. Feelings come and go. They are an indicator of what's in your heart, but your emotions do not define the core of who you are. What you do at home and work is important and even necessary, but what you do will change one day, so make sure your identity rests in your unchanging Savior, Jesus Christ. When your career shifts to another stage, remember whose you are, respect yourself, and serve selflessly.

What others think about you is probably more or less than you deserve, but God knows what's in your heart. You are His precious child, created for doing good. So, do good with and for the Lord. The possessions you enjoy are nice, but they will only have their proper place in your life if Jesus possesses your heart. If all you have disappeared, would your identity fly away with your stuff or would you rest secure as a beloved child of God? In Christ, you are a dearly loved child who walks in the way of love. Be generous with your possessions and you will be free; they will not be able to define you. Who are you? You are a dearly loved child of God who walks in love!

TAKEAWAY: *Relational leaders are free to be who God made them to be.*

Relational Leaders Rest Secure in Their Identity in Christ

Traumatic events like divorce or a job loss can create a crisis of identity. You may have previously parented with a spouse, but now you raise your child alone. As a single parent, you might feel angry, ill-equipped, and financially stressed. Before you were let go from your job, you managed a team and felt respected. After being fired, you struggle just to manage yourself. You might feel unimportant. An identity crisis is an opportunity for Christ to remind you of your identity in Him. "For you died, and your life is now hidden with Christ in God. When *Christ, who is your life*, appears, then you also will appear with him in glory" (Colossians 3:3-4). I am significant in Him, so I am important to Him.

Point to Ponder: The Lord uses what feels out of control to bring His children under His control.

The Lord uses what feels out of control to bring His children under His control. A parent's identity is challenged after a child leaves home as a young adult, just as an individual struggles for significance after retirement. If who we are is wrapped up in what we do, we are bound to experience disillusionment. What we do in life will change, but our standing in Christ remains the same. Our value is not measured by the role we fill but by the abundance of God's grace we enjoy. Relationships are what really count. "Therefore, my brothers and sisters, you whom I love and long for, my joy and crown, stand firm in the Lord in this way, dear friends!" (Philippians 4:1).

Christ Is Your Life

Because Christ is your life, your life is complete. There is no need to strive to be someone you are not, nor is it necessary to reach back and become someone you were that was only relevant for that season of life. The value of your life increases as you proceed to align with Almighty God's character and will for your life. An identity crisis is the Lord's opportunity to take your integrity to another level. You walk securely when integrity instructs your actions.

By God's grace, we must die to the desire to be someone other than God's workmanship in Christ. Rest in your relationship with Jesus and enjoy the people He brings into your life for you to bless. It is the immaterial, not the material, that marks your real worth. Peace of mind, purity of heart, and selfless service make you attractive to be around. As you love the Lord and others, it will be well with your soul.

TAKEAWAY: *Relational leaders rest secure in their identity in Christ.*

Relational Leaders Are Comfortable in Their Own Skin

A popular phrase in today's culture is "you do you," meaning you do what you want to do and I'll do what I want to do, and we will not judge each other. This sounds fair-minded on the surface but is shallow, insufficient, and harmful for followers of Jesus. In Christ, we do what God made us to do by being who God made us to be—our old self has been put to death by belief in Christ's death on the cross for our sins. "For we know that our old self was crucified with him so that the body ruled by sin might be done away with, that we should no longer be slaves to sin—because anyone who has died has been set free from sin" (Romans 6:6-7). He died so we can be set free from the slavery to sin. When we do what God made us to do, we follow the path of humility, holiness, selfless service, and generous living.

> *Point to Ponder:* When I do what God wants me to do, I am the best version of me.

Paul describes slavery to sin as an earthly and eternal bondage experienced by those who seek to be self-reliant and self-sufficient. In Christ, and by God's grace, we acknowledge and accept our death to our old, sin-ridden self, we surrender to our Savior, King Jesus, our new ruler who reigns now and forever. Sin's slavery is the worst imprisonment. It leads to an inferior identity that shuns the freedom of a fulfilling identity in Christ. Sin's slavery is capital punishment for our soul, which becomes shackled and eventually experiences torment in hell. When I do what God wants me to do, I am the best version of me.

Pressure from Others to Be Someone You Are Not

Are you conflicted over being who someone else wants you to be versus being who God desires you to be? Futility and frustration are the bad fruit of attempting to fulfill another's demanding expectations of you. You may meet one of their milestones, but then they raise the bar to a higher level. Thankfully, fulfillment and joy are the good fruit of resting in the Lord's expectations for your life. What does Christ require of you? Waiting and resting may be the remedy the Spirit has for you in contrast to the flesh's propensity to strive out of fear. God's will is not forced, but flows out of His desire for you and others to become more like Jesus. Exchange urgency for trust.

I struggle with needing the approval of others to make me feel valuable and important. But my true self knows that I am already accepted in Christ, so it is ok to say no or offer alternatives to a personal request. As relational leaders, we have to do our best, trust God with the rest, and rest in Him. Be yourself. There will always be another who can do more or less than you, better or worse than you. Know yourself. Know your limits and trust the Lord to fill in the gaps. Allow God's grace and love to grow you into the best version of yourself. Be who God made you to be.

TAKEAWAY: *Relational leaders resist pressure from others to be someone they are not.*

Summary of Chapter Twelve Takeaways

1. Relational leaders are free to be who God made them to be.

2. Relational leaders rest secure in their identity in Christ.

3. Relational leaders resist pressure from others to be someone they are not.

Chapter Thirteen

Be Uniquely Yourself

*I wish that all of you were as I am. But each of you has your
own gift from God; one has this gift, another has that.*

1 Corinthians 7:7

*Always be a first-rate version of yourself, instead
of a second-rate version of somebody else.*

Judy Garland

Being Comfortable with Yourself

Be yourself. Don't strive to be someone else." I received this sage
wisdom from a preaching professor in graduate school. He shared
this advice after we reviewed the six-minute video of my impassioned
talk, in which I resembled a cheap knockoff of the pastor at my home
church—same gestures, same voice inflections, same haircut. It took
years for me to find my own voice, my own unique style of delivering
a talk and being thoroughly comfortable in my own skin. I am learning that, as a relational leader, when *I* am comfortable with me, *others*
are comfortable with me.

Relational Leaders Embrace Their Unique Giftedness

Our generous heavenly Father uniquely gifts His children for His
glory. Like Paul notes, "We have different gifts, according to the grace
given to each of us" (Romans 12:6). We might be given the gift of service, encouragement, teaching, mercy, or administration. Regardless
of one's role, all gifts are necessary in the body of Christ. One may quietly serve as a prayer intercessor behind the scenes, while another may
boldly proclaim truth in front of the faithful. The Lord specially equips

individuals for His good works. God's gift to us is His distinctive stamp of value on each one of us.

> **Point to Ponder:** God's gift to us is His distinctive stamp of value on each one of us.

What do you do well? How can you discover your special realm of service to your Savior Jesus? One way is to develop the abilities that come naturally to you and engage in activities that energize you. The Spirit has wired us in such a way that, when we exercise our gifts, we feel a sense of God's delight in us. Paul puts it this way: "For we are God's handiwork, created in Christ Jesus to do good works, which God prepared in advance for us to do" (Ephesians 2:10). A generous giver finds great joy in giving and an evangelist is ecstatic when they share the gospel. An administrator is not content until everyone and everything is in its place.

You may be an analytical thinker who loves crunching numbers, managing data, and interpreting trends from both. Your gift of linear deduction is critical for business, finance, and engineering. Perhaps you are great with people. People love your company because they sense that you know, understand, and care for them. Thus, your ability to network, convene, and lead others is valuable for accomplishing a big vision or executing a strategic initiative. We must be good stewards of the gifts God has given us!

Seek to marry your passion with your giftedness. For instance, if you love to encourage people and have a way with words, use your gift of writing to convey God's love to their hungry hearts. If you love children, use your ability to nurture and train them in Christ's truth. If you have a teacher's heart and also love sports, use your teaching gift to lead athletes in Bible study. If you love travel, use your aptitude for business to help entrepreneurs here and abroad. Be who God has uniquely gifted you to be!

Heavenly Father, use my gift from You to bring You
glory. Please help me to join my unique giftedness with
pursuits that give me life. In Jesus's name, amen.

TAKEAWAY: *Relational leaders seek to marry their passion with their giftedness.*

Relational Leaders Develop Their Unique Parenting Style

"Dedicate your children to God and point them in the way that they should go, and the values they've learned from you will be with them for life" (Proverbs 22:6 THE PASSION TRANSLATION).

Parenting is not for the faint of heart. Questions related to our child's best interests are like the ocean waves crashing against the seashore of our mind and emotions: how much screen time should we allow? How can we guide kids to choose the best friendships? How are we to balance time between studies, sports, friends, and family? How can we instill foundational Christian values that are embraced and not rejected? How are we to grow a healthy marriage, so that we are able to provide healthy emotional support for our children?

Here are four values I have seen work in our family and in other growing families:

Love

Families are a relational laboratory in how to love others. We experiment, we enjoy successes and endure failures, but all the while we still love each other. Love leads us to think the best about every family member. Love makes us slow to get angry and quick to forgive. Love helps us to be in tune to "emotionally charged" situations like a broken relationship at school, a disappointing test score, failure to make the team, or being misunderstood by a friend. Love helps us to linger long in silence with empathy and an engaged ear. Love is the relational lubricant that allows families to thrive over time. As Paul writes, "For, dear brothers, you have been given freedom: not freedom to do wrong, but freedom to love and serve each other" (Galatians 5:13 TLB).

Honesty

Being honest with what we don't know is a big part of building a healthy family foundation. As Proverbs says, "A good man is guided by his honesty; the evil man is destroyed by his dishonesty" (Proverbs 11:3 TLB). There were many times that I had to apologize to our oldest daughter, Rebekah. "No matter what age you are, I apologize because we've never had a child your age before. We're practicing on you." More than once I have had to go back and say, "I'm sorry. I was impatient. I became angry. Would you forgive me?" I had to be honest about what I didn't know and how I was learning in the process. We're all learning together as a family, so honesty is necessary. Honesty about not knowing what to do often compelled us to pray.

Respect

I really like how my wife, Rita, recently described on the Hindsight podcast the need for respect in a family: "Family has always been really, really important. And respect. You need to respect us, and you need to respect your sisters. Be respectful with their stuff, their space, and respect them as a person. Respect was a really, really big deal with attitudes with words and rolling the eyes an unacceptable kind of disrespect. We really made respect a big priority, which meant we had to model—that's the hard part—and had to say we're sorry a lot. 'We did that wrong' and 'I was disrespectful to you or to Daddy.' Sometimes Boyd has to say, 'I was disrespectful to your mom' and apologize in front of everybody. And that's painful. After you do that a few times, you kind of try to clean up your act a lot more." Respect is a gift we can give to each other, especially during times when respect is undeserved. "Since we *respect* our fathers here on earth, though they punish us, should we not all the more cheerfully submit to God's training so that we can begin really to live?" (Hebrews 12:9 TLB).

Discipline

Discipline is God's design to express love. Consequently, parents who discipline well love well. The wrong form of discipline is destructive and fueled by anger, while constructive discipline is motivated by compassion and instruction. For example, when a child chooses to lie, a loving response by a parent reminds him of the consequences of not telling the truth. Those consequences might entail a lost privilege, an apology to the one deceived, or confession and repentance before God. "*Being punished* isn't enjoyable while it is happening—it hurts! But afterwards we can see the result, a quiet growth in grace and character" (Hebrews 12:11 TLB, emphasis added). Discipline provides needed accountability insofar as it protects us from ourselves and others with nefarious intentions. Lazy parents lack boundaries, while healthy parents are disciplined in their administration of discipline.

> **Point to Ponder:** *Lazy parents lack boundaries, while healthy parents are disciplined in their administration of discipline.*

> *Heavenly Father, I seek Your wisdom to parent each child uniquely and love them all equally. In Jesus's name I pray, amen.*

> **TAKEAWAY:** *Relational leaders parent with rules in order to protect and preserve, but grow intimacy with their children through acceptance and understanding.*

Relational Leaders Honor God Above Themselves

If my story does not promote God, then I am only promoting myself. Pride has a way of making me the central character in my story instead of Christ. For example, in describing my Christian conversion, do I exalt the Lord, or do I draw too much attention to myself? The remedy for self-promotion and self-praise is exaltation of Almighty God in grateful praise and worship. Gratitude for God's grace puts pride in its place. If not for His relentless love, I would be unsaved and undone. Shameless gratitude to Jesus keeps Jesus the main character in my story!

> **Point to Ponder:** *Pride has a way of making me the central character in my story instead of Christ.*

Paul—who had quite a story—kept the focus on the eternal King Jesus. In an explosive doxology, he declares honor and glory to the only immortal, invisible, and incorruptible God of the universe. "Now to the King eternal, immortal, invisible, the only God, be honor and glory for ever and ever. Amen" (1 Timothy 1:17). We are but a speck of sand on the seashore of the Trinity's creation. In our mother's womb we were a gleam in the eye of our creative heavenly Father.

Relational Leaders Boast in the Lord's Accomplishments, Not Their Own

Lost in our sins, we were the object of Christ's eternal affection as He suffered on the cross. In need of care and comfort, we are led and loved by the invisible and insightful Holy Spirit. Thus, we humbly bow in thankful praise to God for His blessings so that we might boast in Him alone! "It is because of him that you are in Christ Jesus, who has become for us wisdom from God—that is, our righteousness, holiness and redemption. Therefore, as it is written: 'Let the one who boasts boast in the Lord'" (1 Corinthians 1:30-31).

What are some ways to praise the Lord? Certainly in our prayer time we can praise Him with our favorite hymn or worship song or we can read out loud and praise the Lord with His Word, perhaps with a passage like Psalm 145. Praise God at church with fellow believers in singing together, in reading the Bible together, in celebration of baptism together, and corporately remembering Jesus's sacrifice for our sins through sacred communion. Praise God from whom all blessings flow!

What does it mean to praise God? To praise the Lord is to thank Him and give Him the honor and glory due His name. The Almighty is worthy of praise because of His greatness, His goodness, and His glory! When we prayerfully weigh every word we speak, we praise Jesus with the fruit of our lips. Humility is the Holy Spirit's homing device to point people to Christ and not exalt ourselves. All creation cries out in praise—how much more should we praise the Lord's crowning achievement by declaring His holy name. Praise keeps God in His preeminent place.

As the writer of Hebrews puts it: "Through Jesus, therefore, let us continually offer to God a sacrifice of praise—the fruit of lips that openly profess his name. And do not forget to do good and to share with others, for with such sacrifices God is pleased" (Hebrews 13:15-16).

TAKEAWAY: *Relational leaders boast in the Lord's accomplishments, not their own.*

Summary of Chapter Thirteen Takeaways

1. Relational leaders seek to marry their passion with their giftedness.
2. Relational leaders parent with rules in order to protect and preserve, but grow intimacy with their children through acceptance and understanding.
3. Relational leaders boast in the Lord's accomplishments, not their own.

Chapter Fourteen

Connect Good People
with Good People

*I commend to you Phoebe our sister, who is a servant of the church
in order that you may receive her in the Lord in a manner worthy
of the saints, and assist her in whatever business she has need of
you; for indeed she has been a helper of many and of myself also.*

ROMANS 16:1-2 NKJV

*You can have everything in life you want if you will
just help enough other people get what they want.*

ZIG ZIGLAR

Relational Leaders Are Relationally Generous

Making introductions is one of the richest forms of relational giving. Entrusting two people I know to each other for the purpose of them getting to know one another is a true gift. My willingness to use my influence to bring together two people for the sake of a growing relationship can be a fruitful investment. I am a much richer person today because friends have unselfishly introduced me to their friends over the years. Many times I have gained a new friend who became a messenger of Christ for me. Relational giving is a catalyst for God's will. Jesus works through people.

> **Point to Ponder:** Making introductions is one of the richest forms of relational giving.

Paul was open-handed with his loyal friend Epaphroditus: "Therefore I am all the more eager to send [Epaphroditus], so that when you see him again you may be glad and I may have less anxiety. So then, welcome him in the Lord with great joy, and honor people like him, because he almost died for the work of Christ" (Philippians 2:28-30). His love for his brother, coworker, and fellow soldier in the faith did not keep Paul from sharing this stellar servant of the Lord with other saints in need. Though Paul suffered in a Roman prison, he willingly commissioned his trusted friend to serve other friends at a church hundreds of miles away in Philippi. Paul implored those benefiting from Epaphroditus's sacrifice to welcome him in the Lord joyfully. Grateful recipients of relational generosity honor the gift and the giver.

What friend or acquaintance needs an introduction to someone you know? Someone suffering from an emotional or physical illness may need an introduction to a doctor you know who specializes in their area of pain. A friend who is out of work could use your recommendation to a company that you know is hiring. Maybe you need to release a relationship for a season so that your friend can serve the Lord in another part of the world. Relational generosity is risky. Things may not work out, and someone may get hurt. Your part is to obey and patiently trust God to work out His will.

> **TAKEAWAY:** *Relational leaders take the risk of introducing others, even if things don't work out.*

Generous Relational Leaders Prosper and Refresh Others and Themselves

"One person gives freely, yet gains even more; another withholds unduly, but comes to poverty. A generous person will prosper; whoever refreshes others will be refreshed" (Proverbs 11:24-25). I have not met a generous leader who was not prosperous. These leaders have not always been prosperous financially, but certainly relationally, emotionally, and spiritually. Giving leaders tend to be rich in what matters most. I am reminded of a couple of leaders that sponsor individuals and families to attend the Generous Giving Conference. Annually, they invest thousands of dollars in 50 new people whom they know will be touched by the Spirit to grow in their generosity. Jess and Angela find great joy in helping others discover refreshment in generous living. Leaders prosper and are refreshed when they help others do the same.

> **Point to Ponder:** *You prosper and are refreshed when you help others do the same.*

God's economy is counterintuitive to conventional wisdom. Proverbs teaches that a generous person who gives freely is entrusted by God with more, while a stingy person who holds on forfeits his opportunity to gain more from the Lord. God cannot place blessings in the palm of a hand that is balled up into a greedy fist. But He finds great joy in giving to those who allow blessings to pass through their open hands. Generosity produces prosperity and refreshment. As Paul says, "Remember this: Whoever sows sparingly will also reap sparingly, and whoever sows generously will also reap generously" (2 Corinthians 9:6).

Do you look for opportunities to be generous with your time, money, wisdom and relationships? Does your generous giving enrich you and empower others to be generous givers? What you give for God's kingdom is a secure investment with an eternal return. Remember those who took the time to teach and mentor you professionally, spiritually, in marriage, and in parenting. Pray about whom you can walk alongside and help them grow from your mistakes and learning what success really looks like. Like a cold glass of homemade lemonade on a summer day—you will refresh others and be refreshed yourself!

Spend time preparing a generosity plan, just as you would create a business plan. Budget your time to be with others for intentional mentoring, coaching, or consulting. Your generosity plan may include a percentage of your business revenue in your giving fund at National Christian Foundation, an annual one percent increase in your giving from your personal budget, or seeding a giving fund for your children to start practicing the habit of generous giving. Most of all, be generous with your time, sitting quietly before the Lord!

TAKEAWAY: *Relational leaders are generous in their coaching and connecting of other leaders.*

My Friend David—Not Your Normal Certified Public Accountant

David called me one day and wanted to introduce me to Chris and Teri. "They are on the other line, can you talk?" "Sure," I said. Chris and Teri had just sold their business and were considering their giving and serving options in this exciting new season of life. Like a runner in a relay race, David handed off the relational baton and never looked back. He knew the power of connecting two couples who could complement each other with their experiences and expertise. As a result of David's generosity, my wife and I have grown our friendship over the past eight years with this incredibly generous couple through travel, serving on ministry boards, and attending generosity conferences.

Point to Ponder: Be bold to connect others when they transition into a new season of life.

A Process to Gain Access and Influence with People You Want to Know

The National Association for Stock Car Auto Racing (NASCAR) has one of the most loyal and rabid fan bases, people who have been deeply influenced by the sport's intoxicating effect. Though I am not a fan, I am amazed by those who are enamored by the sport's entertaining allure. An innovate ministry leader in this industry was in my office last year, and she educated me in how she builds relationships at raceway sporting events and, in the process, earns the right to share the gospel. What a creative way to go to the people, get to know them, so they might come to know Jesus!

Blogger Amy Martin describes the process of how NASCAR leaders have built their fan base:

- Access leads to connection. (Fans are able to sign the actual racetrack.)
- Connection leads to relationships. (At all ages.)
- Relationships lead to affinity. (You can't fake this affinity.)
- Affinity leads to influence. (There's a reason so many brands are attracted to NASCAR.)
- Influence leads to conversion. (These fans would likely buy anything this driver is selling.)

(Page 48, *How to Win Friends and Influence People in the Digital Age* by Dale Carnegie and Associates.)

As we learn how to love like Jesus and enjoy access with Him, we can apply this process of influencing others with our everyday relationships and with new friends we would like to meet. Below, I've applied the NASCAR process of developing devoted fans to our influence of others.

Access Leads to Connection

Similar to a NASCAR fan inviting an acquaintance to a race for the first time, you could invite someone you would like to know better to an experience you both would enjoy: a sporting event, training seminar, men or women's conference, a concert, church, golf, tennis, hiking, or a business opportunity. Be willing and generous to invest time and money to grow relational equity. When you give people access to your life, interests, and relationships you grow understanding and trust.

Several years ago, I hoped to meet a leader who led a family foundation in south Florida. We had a mutual friend who agreed to set up a meeting for us to get to know one another. It turned out that another friend of mine and I had served our new acquaintance's father several years before at a mountain resort. This common experience solidified our connection.

Connection Leads to Relationships

The leader of the family foundation, whom I'll call Scott, asked thoughtful questions that revealed his interest in our best practices certification for nonprofits and a willingness to personally engage in our year-long program. Over the next 12 months, we were able to build a relationship during our monthly shared experience of teaching, training, and coaching. Growing a relationship takes intentionality.

Relationships are like a tender seedling—they require attention and care. Each person waters with time and cultivates with understanding. Over time, the relationship takes root and eventually bears fruit. This leads us to the next progression in gaining influence: relationships lead to affinity.

Relationships Lead to Affinity

What exactly is affinity? Affinity is "sympathy marked by community of interest," according to *Merriam-Webster's*. Dedication to a common interest increases the likelihood for two people to grow closer to one another by getting to know each other. An excuse to hang out together over a worthwhile project grows affinity.

Scott and I both were passionate about helping faith-based ministries build organizational capacity so that they could most effectively further their God-given mission and vision. We experimented on an executive leadership group model that proved to be a most valuable collaborative process in which leaders could exchange ideas, resources, and relationships. Scott's foundation generously provided scholarships, and we were able to provide leadership. I knew our affinity had solidified the moment we celebrated our results and discovered ways to improve.

Affinity Leads to Influence

Because I trusted and respected Scott, I was very open to his input on how to make our best practices training and coaching even better. I felt the same trust and respect from him. Scott was very interested in our organizational growth plan and the financial and human resources required to advance to the next level. Our shared interest grew our interest in each other.

Now you might feel like you don't have a year to grow affinity with another person or organization—you need help now! I truly feel your angst, but part of the shift in learning to love like Jesus is to think about rich relationships in the long-term, not the short-term. We must trust that God's timing is best for everyone, and we need to guard against using people for our own agenda and having only shallow interest in theirs. Long-term relationships expand influence.

Influence Leads to Conversion

Another way to communicate the notion that influence can lead to conversion is that influence can lead to becoming a raving fan. Because of the generosity and practical wisdom of Scott and his family, our team became raving fans of their passion and priorities as a foundation. Instead of just looking to our interests (which we were compelled to follow), we learned how to appreciate the value of what a third-generation organization like his had to offer. By taking time to learn from them, we were able to educate them in the ideas that we had developed over the years. Everyone was better for the arrangement and connection. *We* is better than *me*!

Three years into our relationship, Scott casually asked me one day how his foundation could make a significant investment into Ministry Ventures (which, by God's grace, I cofounded in 1999). I explained our vision to repurpose our content for an online learning platform, which resonated with his entrepreneurial DNA. Over the following three years, after improving our plan with the foundation's input, they gave a significant six-figure gift to Ministry Ventures to practice what we preached about innovation and growth. The results were stunning, and their gift reaped a harvest tenfold what they invested!

Relational conversion may be an individual coming to faith because of your influence, or it might mean that an organization enjoys favor from God and people because of your faithfulness to invest for the long-term.

TAKEAWAY: *Relational leaders follow a process of pouring into others without expecting anything in return.*

Summary of Chapter Fourteen Takeaways

1. Relational leaders take the risk of introducing others, even if things don't work out.

2. Relational leaders are generous in their coaching and connecting of other leaders.

3. Relational leaders follow a process of pouring into others without expecting anything in return.

Chapter Fifteen

Be Loved by God to Love for God

*You yourselves are our letter, written on our hearts, known and read
by everyone. You show that you are a letter from Christ, the result
of our ministry, written not with ink but with the Spirit of the
living God, not on tablets of stone but on tablets of human hearts.*

2 Corinthians 3:2-3

*The Bible is God's "love letter" to us, telling us not only that He
loves us, but showing us what He has done to demonstrate His
love. It also tells us how we should live, because God knows what
is best for us and He wants us to experience it. Never forget: The
Bible is God's Word, given to us so we can know and follow Him.*

Billy Graham

Jesus's Intimacy with His Father Flowed from Oneness with His Father

Jesus is God. He claimed oneness with His heavenly Father to His disciples: "I and the Father are one" (John 10:30). When they saw Jesus, they saw the Father. He displayed His divinity with His perfect character. He validated His status as Savior and Lord by His miracles. His clear public teaching of His equality with God brought out the wrath of the religious leaders. His elevation to Deity in the minds of mere mortals was a threat to the reigning monarchs of men. Christ is in God and God is in Christ.

Since Jesus is in the Father and the Father in Jesus, by faith we are in Christ and Christ is in us. This is a mystery of the Christian life: that the fullness of God lives within all who embrace Jesus as God. When we said "I do" to our Savior, we vowed that He was everything He claimed to be. Our groom, Christ, desires us to grow in grace each day through oneness with Him. Just as He prayed: "That all of them may be one, Father, just as you are in me and I am in you. May they also be in us so that the world may believe that you have sent me. I have given them the glory that you gave me, that they may be one as we are one—I in them and you in me—so that they may be brought to complete unity. Then the world will know that you sent me and have loved them even as you have loved me" (John 17:21-23). Our unity with the triune God means that love is manifest in our life. Christ, who is in us, transforms us into His loving likeness. As Paul says, "So then, just as you received Christ Jesus as Lord, continue to live your lives in him, rooted and built up in him, strengthened in the faith as you were taught, and overflowing with thankfulness" (Colossians 2:6-7).

What Does It Mean for a Relational Leader to Be Intimate with Christ?

When people see you, do they see Jesus? Is your soul so surrendered to your Savior that what comes from your inner being is beautiful to behold? A soul submitted to Christ loves like Christ. A mind saturated with the thoughts of Christ thinks like Christ. A heart filled with the character of Christ behaves like Christ. As Paul writes, "My goal is that they may be encouraged in heart and united in love, so that they may have the full riches of complete understanding, in order that they may know the mystery of God, namely, Christ, in whom are hidden all the treasures of wisdom and knowledge" (Colossians 2:2-3). A life aligned with the Lord is one with His will. Thus, we trust that Christ is God and spend a lifetime learning what it means, and He changes us the whole way through. We believe and then we are able to see. Our next step of trust in Jesus shows us more of Jesus!

Heavenly intimacy provides opportunities to grow our earthly intimacies. Our heart for Christ grows our heart for people, our love for Christ expands our love for people, and our service for Christ extends to selfless service for people. The Lord's love letter to us gives us ideas and images of how to see people as God does. The Holy Spirit inscribes love on the hearts of people we have ministered to in the name of Jesus.

Point to Ponder: Intimacy with the Almighty grows our faith and love in order to serve others with an expanded capacity to trust and love.

TAKEAWAY: *Relational leaders with a heart filled with the love of Christ love like Christ.*

The Motivation and Manner of Our Love for Others

We are called to love others because of our heavenly Father's great love for us. Almighty God loves with an incredible love. His love has no boundaries or bias. The love of Jesus is limitless to the extent to which He will give us His grace. His love goes behind the enemy's lines of deceit and rescues those lost in their loveless state of mind. Christ's love looks for the unloved and offers comfort, care, compassion, and forgiveness.

Jesus modeled loving people regardless of their "emotional baggage" or spiritual unbelief. He forgave a woman caught in adultery and admonished her to sin no more. He cared for society's outcast—a female Samaritan—by offering her the "Living Water" of Himself. He patiently taught an inquisitive but fearful religious leader—Nicodemus—of the need to be born again by the cleansing water of heavenly grace. Jesus modeled for His disciples how they were to love one another by the way He cared for them with menial, but very meaningful, tasks of service. Whom do you know who is caught in sin, who needs you through your love to teach them of their freedom in Christ?

Point to Ponder: Patient love is able to point people to Jesus as the object of its deep love and affection.

Why does the Almighty love you with such abandonment? One reason is so that you can be a catalyst for Christ's love. You have the inconceivable opportunity to love others on behalf of the Lord. While a friend or family member may writhe in physical agony or emotional pain, you are an extension of God's eternal love on earth, because you are extremely loved by God. As 1 John puts it, "We love because he first loved us" (1 John 4:19). You have His extra love to administer to others' loneliness and to their frantic fears.

Love is not received to be stored up in your soul like a savings account; rather, it is to be paid forward to neighbors, work associates, and enemies. Love is quick to forgive and slow to criticize. It looks for ways to bless those whose last blessing is long gone. Love grows a relationship into a beautiful garden of green plants, deep-rooted trees, and the tantalizing smell of luscious flowers.

Love does not sit still, but searches out souls in need of its care. Take time to regularly receive the love of Jesus into your life. Commune with Christ, the lover of your soul, and you will experience His peace and security. When your spirit is rested, you share love robustly with another hungry heart. As we read in 1 John, "God is love. Whoever lives in love lives in God, and God in them" (1 John 4:16). Enter into God's eternal love so you can share it. The Lord loves you so you can love on others. As Paul writes, "But we ought always to thank God for you, brothers and sisters loved by the Lord, because God chose you as firstfruits to be saved through the sanctifying work of the Spirit and through belief in the truth" (2 Thessalonians 2:13).

> **Point to Ponder:** As we love others like Jesus loves them, this becomes a habit of our hearts.

We Are Compelled to Love Others When We Lift Them to the Lord in Prayer

Occasionally I find myself thinking bad thoughts about another person, and at times I get downright angry at someone's insensitivity toward me or someone I care about. Only when I pray for them am I prepared to love them like the Lord loves them. I have to ask myself the following question: "Though I have been hurt by this person, how by the power of the Holy Spirit can I look beyond my hurt to the healing their heart needs?" In Jesus's name, I can pray for wholeness of soul for the both of us. My posture of prayer prepares me to let go of my hang-ups and lift up a needy soul in love.

> **TAKEAWAY:** *Relational leaders pray for others who are hard to love so that it's hard not to love them.*

Four Ways to Love God

Love is the most powerful weapon in our arsenal of faith. Jesus commands our love of God: "Love the Lord your God with all your heart and with all your soul and with all your mind and with all your strength" (Mark 12:30). Like the tip of an arrow, love points us to God. Love commandeers all other energies to engage the Lord's affection and His eternal concerns. When Jesus defined love as the greatest command, He gave us a glimpse into what He wants for the world and His children. A life motivated by love is only limited by its capacity to love the Lord. Love is a muscle we exercise so it grows in stamina and strength. Here are four ideas to develop our love for God:

Love God with Your Emotions

Jesus starts at the heart of the matter—our heart. Our heart is the seat of our feelings and affections. Our heart captures our passions and yearnings. We are drawn to what we desire, what we value. Yes, the heart follows what it treasures above all else. In the same way an engaged person fervently seeks to engage the heart of their lover, so also as the the bride of Christ we passionately pursue His heart. As our heart loves Jesus, He simultaneously settles and stirs our emotions. The psalmist exhorts us to love God with our whole hearts: "Trust in him at all times, you people; pour out your hearts to him, for God is our refuge" (Psalm 62:8).

Love God with Your Soul

In the beginning, God breathed life into the soul of man (Genesis 2:7). Our soul is our entire being brought into existence by the Spirit of the Lord. It is here, deep within the recesses of our spirit, that we commune with Christ. Our marriage to Jesus was consummated when, by grace through faith, He saved our soul. Prayer is our bedchamber of intimacy for us to love our Lord with all our soul. Christ is our companion and confidant. A soul in love with God seeks God by faith. "As the deer pants for streams of water, so my soul pants for you, my God" (Psalm 42:1).

Love God with Your Mind

A mind in love with the Lord wants to do the Lord's will. In the same way that a noble idea captures our imagination so much that it drastically influences our actions, so to know and do God's will is the goal of those in love with Jesus. Mental romancing with the mind of Christ marks the thoughts of those who trust and obey. Knowledge of God acquired out of love starves our pride and feeds our humility. Big, worshipful God thoughts expand our love for our sovereign Lord. "'What no eye has seen, what no ear has heard, and what no human mind has conceived'—these things God has prepared for those who love him" (1 Corinthians 2:9).

Love God with Your Strength

Energy in eternal matters is what matters most. When our focused attention is on the important things (like giving) and not the trivial things (like worry) we thrive in our love for the Lord. What activity may be competing with your time with Christ? Avoid activities that create sideways energy. Our strength increases as we engage with other followers of Jesus who are on fire for Him. Like a bonfire ignited by gasoline, so the prayers and encouragement of God's people fan our fire of faith and love for God. Being around people in love with Jesus grows our love for Jesus. As the psalmist writes, "I love you, LORD, my strength" (Psalm 18:1).

TAKEAWAY: *Relational leaders are loved by the Lord so that they can love the Lord and partner with God in loving others.*

Summary of Chapter Fifteen Takeaways

1. Relational leaders with a heart filled with the love of Christ love like Christ.

2. Relational leaders pray for others who are hard to love so that it's hard not to love them.

3. Relational leaders are loved by the Lord so that they can love the Lord and partner with God in loving others.

Chapter Sixteen

Influence Influencers

The [instructions] which you have heard from me along with many witnesses, transmit and entrust [as a deposit] to reliable and faithful men who will be competent and qualified to teach others also.

2 TIMOTHY 2:2 AMPC

Influence is when you are not the one talking and yet your words fill the room; when you are absent and yet your presence is felt everywhere.

TEMITOPE IBRAHIM

Jesus Influenced Influencers

Nicodemus came to Jesus at night and said, "Rabbi, we know that you are a teacher who has come from God" (John 3:2). Nicodemus was a respected leader of the Pharisees during the day and a curious seeker of the Jewish Savior at night. Some start their quest for Christ discreetly. Quietly they read a book about God or seek Him in the confines of a church or cathedral. Those who are simply curious about Christ are not ready to follow Him in faith, but they are open to learning more about Jesus. For fear of being made fun of by their unbelieving friends, they may hide their faith experiment. Nonetheless, like a moth moves toward light, they draw closer to God's warm love.

> **Point to Ponder:** Invest in those who can influence others for Jesus.

Nicodemus was curious about Christ. He came to see Jesus by night for fear of being found out by his friends. Like many today, he acknowledged that Jesus was a gifted teacher from God but did not accept Him as God. Yes, our Lord taught as no one else: with authority, clarity, and humility. He taught beautifully and boldly. "The people were amazed at his teaching, because [Jesus] taught them as one who had authority, not as the teachers of the law" (Mark 1:22). However, His teaching was not an end, but a means to reveal a person's need to believe in Him as their Lord and Savior. Christ taught them to trust in Him.

Relational Leaders Influence Influencers for Christ

Are you just curious about Christ, or do you really want to know Him in a trusting relationship? Do you secretly seek Him or do you publicly profess Him? Curiosity about Christ is not enough, unless it leads to conversion to Christ. Curiosity can create a circumstance that educates and allows the Holy Spirit to draw a heart to Himself. Seek to learn more about the Lord so you can know the Lord. Knowing the Lord is not a sterile intellectual exercise that tickles the mind, but a spiritual transformation of your heart. Engage in curiosity to move you closer to God, not further from God.

Curiosity can lead to conversion. Nicodemus eventually went public with his faith. He defended Christ to his peers and he accompanied Joseph to request and prepare the body of Jesus for burial. Be patient with those who are curious in their faith. Be a catalyst for them to grow in their spiritual understanding by pointing them back to the study of Scripture. Pray with them, pray for them, and support them in their search for God. Curiosity about Christ can lead to Christ.

"Then Agrippa said to Paul, 'Do you think that in such a short time you can persuade me to be a Christian?'" (Acts 26:28).

Heavenly Father, use my curiosity about
Christ to grow my faith in Christ.

TAKEAWAY: *Relational leaders help influencers grow in their spiritual understanding by pointing them back to the study of Scripture.*

A Global Influencer of Influencers

"In the year that King Uzziah died, I saw the Lord, high and exalted, seated on a throne; and the train of his robe filled the temple...Then I heard the voice of the Lord saying, 'Whom shall I send? And who will go for us?' And I said, 'Here am I. Send me!'" (Isaiah 6:1, 8)

Ever since I became a Christian in 1979 as a freshman in college, Billy Graham has been in my life as a mentor, friend, and model of how to follow Christ. As a very zealous young convert with a fiery heart for the Lord, I tried to read and listen to everything Billy wrote or said and added into my reading diet what others wrote about him for good measure. His sermons became my quiet time reflections and templates for my talks. I met him once in his twilight before his Atlanta Crusade in 1994, and since we were in the pre-selfie era, I missed out on a photo, but shook his warm hand and felt his loving heart. My eyes said to his blue eyes: "I love and admire you—thank you." Billy's recent transition to heaven is God's gain and my loss, but his influence on me will never be forgotten.

Billy Graham Was Humble

Billy never forgot where he came from. I don't just mean his humble beginnings on a dairy farm, but his spiritual bankruptcy before his faith in Christ. Hands clasped together and head bowed in reverent posture, he petitioned heaven for lost souls to be saved. Prayer, he said, more than his preaching, was the conduit for the Father to draw sinners to faith and repentance. His humility to maintain a simple life of love for the Lord and people kept life's clutter at bay.

In addition, his humility led him to be accountable with his finances, and he kept his modest salary at arm's length, thereby avoiding any conflict of interest. Humility also breeds wisdom. He ascribed early on to an ethic of not allowing himself to be alone with another woman so as to not even have an appearance of misconduct or any career-ending scenario of "he said, she said." My friend, who is a relative of Billy's, told me a few years ago, "Billy can call anyone on the planet and they will answer his call, but he is so humble, he is not even aware of his lofty influence." Billy's humility reminds me to take myself less seriously and the Lord's agenda more seriously.

> **Point to Ponder:** *Humility reminds me to take myself less seriously and the Lord's agenda more seriously.*

Billy Graham Was Bold

Billy Graham was bold, not brash. He was bold in the power of the Holy Spirit. Because God was his audience of one and the Bible was the basis of his authoritative message, he would share the good news of Jesus to paupers, princes, and everyone in between. He had no need to apologize, nor was he ever ashamed, because he knew in his heart that the gospel was the power of God unto salvation (Romans 1:16) and that there is no other name [Jesus] under heaven whereby humankind must be saved (Acts 4:12)! It is refreshing to see someone without airs raise his Bible in the air and call on all cultures to confess Christ. Billy's boldness challenges me to have a sense of urgency to see as many people as possible be saved.

Billy Graham Was a Person of Love

Very similarly to the apostle Paul, Billy was compelled by the love of Christ to love on behalf of Christ. Because the Lord's love had lifted him out of the miry pit of pride and unbelief, he was ever grateful to proclaim the grace of God that offered authentic life and liberty through faith in Jesus. His pure love for the Lord, for his family, and for people motivated him to travel the world and, in some cases, confine himself to bed rest during the day to rest and reflect so that he might have the energy to engage massive audiences at night. Because God loved him as a lost sinner, he was able to love sinners and show them how to find the love of their life—Jesus. Billy's love was a bright light illuminated by his capacity to receive God's love into his heart. I too want to love like Billy loved!

Billy Graham Is Receiving His Reward

Billy Graham was a man. He is not to be worshiped but admired. His example motivates us. Just as Isaiah lost a hero in King Uzziah, so all of us who are branded by Jesus miss our friend and hero Billy. And like Isaiah, we say, "Here we are, Lord, send us in Your power to share the gospel of Jesus with a heart of humility and a boldness based on the Bible and a life of love." Billy was the quintessential "good and faithful servant." I can only imagine he is next door to Mother Teresa, and I look forward to hanging out with them one day. But in the meantime, let's rescue the perishing!

Heavenly Father, grow me into a faithful follower of Jesus
like Your faithful servants before me. In Jesus's name, amen.

TAKEAWAY: *Relational leaders aspire to be like those who have a track record of loving and leading well.*

Audience with Influencers

Are you developing your God-given gifts? Are you sharpening your skills as a responsible steward? You have everything you need to become what Christ intends for your life, but it requires growth and development. People who sit on their hands, satisfied at their current level of competency, make me sad. Only those who stretch themselves and continue to advance experience God's best. "Do you see a man skilled in his work? He will serve before kings; he will not serve before obscure men" (Proverbs 22:29 NASB).

Why only reminisce over past blessings when you can attain new milestones? Influencers want to be around fresh thinkers who are constantly growing in their character. Smart leaders surround themselves with other servant leaders who never stop learning. Perhaps you take the time to sharpen your skills and thus create value that is attractive to those in authority. It could be a continuing education class in computers, a master's level course in business, or an in-depth Bible study. Skills need development.

> **Point to Ponder:** Sharpen your skills so you can serve those with influence.

Relational Leaders Use Their Skills for Positive Influence

The Lord gives you wisdom to use your skills in strategic service (see Exodus 28:2). Ask Him where to invest your attributes and aptitudes for the highest kingdom impact. Don't remain in mediocrity when you can be a man or woman of excellence who serves an incredibly influential visionary leader. Consider leaving your comfortable place of employment for a challenging assignment with Christ. Like exercised muscles, skills need to be stretched by faith. God's will advances when we embrace the tension of trust and obedience.

Skilled servants of the Lord have a lasting impact on a hurting world. Invest your time with integrity and the absence of ego. Be like Huram, who "was highly skilled and experienced in all kinds of bronze work. He came to King Solomon and did all the work assigned to him" (1 Kings 7:14). Be content behind the scenes, knowing the investment of your expert advice is influencing the decision-maker. An ingenious and industrious person exercises influence with influencers. Ask yourself, "for what significant leader can I leverage the skills given me by my Lord in this season of service?"

> **TAKEAWAY:** Relational leaders offer their expert advice behind the scenes to influence a decision-maker.

Summary of Chapter Sixteen Takeaways

1. Relational leaders help influencers grow in their spiritual

understanding by pointing them back to the study of Scripture.

2. Relational leaders aspire to be like those who have a track record of loving and leading well.

3. Relational leaders offer their expert advice behind the scenes to influence a decision-maker.

Chapter Seventeen

Look for Daily
Divine Appointments

It was necessary for [Jesus] to go through Samaria.

JOHN 4:4 AMPC

To every soul that knows how to pray, to every soul that by faith comes to Jesus, the true mercy seat, divine sovereignty wears no dark and terrible aspect but is full of love.

CHARLES SPURGEON

Jesus on Mission

Then Jesus was led by the Spirit into the wilderness to be tempted by the devil" (Matthew 4:1). What? Jesus was led by the Spirit to have an appointment with the devil? Yes! And having anticipated the enemy's schemes and tricks, Jesus struck back with the Word of God. Divine appointments do not always feel divine, but they have a divine purpose. Jesus understood that He was on mission to accomplish His heavenly Father's heart. Christ looked for where the Lord was at work, showed up, and went to work for God's glory.

Relational Leaders Look for Divine Appointments

Look for divine appointments daily. A divine appointment is a Spirit-orchestrated encounter with people who need our attention or with people from whom we need love and correction. Already scheduled by the Holy Spirit with eternal purpose, our part is to pray and discern God's will. With his calendar written on our heart, Christ waits for us to follow, even when we feel uncomfortable. Divine appointments have a much broader purpose.

When I hired a strength coach two years ago, I thought that the primary purpose was for my physical well-being. I quickly learned that the Lord's greater game plan was for my new friend's soul. Don and I have become good friends, and we respect each other's expertise and experience. Don coaches me with a well thought-through exercise routine and just as much focus on the best nutritional intake. And I help Don grow in his understanding of Scripture and salvation in Jesus. He just suggested we meet monthly for dinner and savory discussions!

> **Point to Ponder:** A divine appointment is a Spirit-orchestrated encounter with people who need our love.

Christ connects us with people for His unique purposes. It could be an occasion to meet someone for the very first time, or it may be a casual acquaintance or a familiar friend. Regardless of the relational connection, it is important to ask the Lord how to bless the one in our presence and be open to receive a blessing from them.

Our calendar of appointments can become a prayer list for us to ask for wisdom from God as we seek to serve others over a meal, coffee, or in a meeting. It's uncanny how we can find ourselves in need and our Savior sends someone that becomes His hands and feet of faith and hope. They provide a kind and encouraging word or an insight that gives us courage and direction to do the right thing. Thank God for His inspiring ambassadors!

Christ-Centered Collaboration

When you collaborate with a coworker, do you see them through the eyes of Christ? If so, you might perceive from their past a frightened five-year-old whose parents divorced, or now, an insecure adult whose identity is tied to what they do instead of who they are. It's in face-to-face encounters that you are able to express your faith with compassion. Hurting, hard hearts desire Jesus when they know they have been cared for like Jesus.

Watch for God to orchestrate opportunities for you to introduce His love. Anyone you encounter throughout the day is a candidate for your intentional interest. Your neighbor, hairstylist, cashier, server, vendor, and mechanic need your smile. People are not a vending machine waiting for a transaction to be taken; rather, they are created in the image of God waiting for someone to show them His grace and truth.

Someone may be startled by, or even suspect of, your interest in their life—prepare for this, but do not allow another's hesitant heart to keep you from extending genuine comfort. You never know how the seed of a kind word, a listening ear, a practical idea, or an encouraging prayer will germinate and grow in one seeking soul. Divine appointments are much bigger than your agenda—so try to see daily encounters through the lens of eternity. Ask yourself, "How can I each day prayerfully discern the divine appointments God sends my way?"

> **TAKEAWAY:** *Relational leaders look for divine appointments.*

An Illustration, Not an Interruption

One morning in my prayer chair at home, my precious 7-year-old grandbaby Lily "caught" me reading and praying the Psalms. Instead of being glad that she saw me, her Pop, reading the Bible, I was a little annoyed my time with God had been "interrupted." She crawled up into my lap, and suddenly my heavenly Father reminded me, "This is not an interruption, but an illustration of my love, care, and affection for you, son." My heart warmed, and then I noticed several bruises on her sun-soaked legs, the evidence of an active child. The Holy Spirit whispered, "Boyd, you are bruised and broken, and I Am your Comforter and Healer." Peace, joy, confidence, hope, faith, and love, all at once—moved me closer to Christ. Jesus illustrated through an "interruption" what I was seeking all along—His loving presence.

> *Point to Ponder: Jesus sometimes illustrates through "interruptions" what we were seeking all along—His loving presence.*

The unnamed foreigner—a Samaritan woman—was minding her own business when a stranger interrupted her domestic duties of drawing water from the refreshing well: "The Samaritan woman said to him, 'You are a Jew and I am a Samaritan woman. How can you ask me for a drink?' (For Jews do not associate with Samaritans.) Jesus answered her, 'If you knew the gift of God and who it is that asks you for a drink, you would have asked him and he would have given you living water'" (John 4:9-10). Jesus asked her for a favor—a drink of water—but the larger purpose was for the Lord to give this searching, hardworking adult—created in the image of God—living water for her thirsty soul. The Messiah she had heard about was in her presence to offer her the satisfaction of His forgiveness and love.

Traffic, a sick child, a costly home repair, a long line, a needy neighbor, a complaining customer, a late vendor, or a coworker in crisis may seem like interruptions. But they are not. Look for an illustration of God's character in your disruptive circumstances. When you encounter a person in sorrow, imagine Christ on the cross when He sought comfort from His heavenly Father. Interruptions are appointments for compassion, like when Jairus came to Jesus seeking healing for his daughter: "Jairus came, and when he saw Jesus, he fell at his feet. He pleaded earnestly with him, 'My little daughter is dying. Please come and put your hands on her so that she will be healed and live.' So, Jesus went with him" (Mark 5:22-24). In your everyday routine, recognize the Lord in the little things and love like your Savior Jesus. "Interruptions" are simply people to love.

Loving people is the business of believers in God. That "business" might be loving a person in your immediate presence or an individual in your peripheral vision; it could be a restaurant server who needs to be included in your prayer when you thank the Lord for your meal. Your "business" loving might lead you to a doctor or nurse that cares for you or a loved one who needs to be encouraged, or perhaps a critic that doesn't have the full story, who needs patience and grace. Look for illustrations of God's works at work, at home, on vacation—but especially in your interruptions. Let interruptions slow you down to better focus on faith in God.

*Heavenly Father, open my eyes of faith to see Your
illustrations of faith in my life's interruptions.*

TAKEAWAY: Relational leaders see the Lord working through life's interruptions.

Relational Leaders Embrace "God Detours" as a Better Way

Sometimes the Lord directs me down a different road from where I thought I was going. In the same way an orange detour sign's black arrow points drivers around an impassable road, so the Spirit can lead me in a circuitous route to avoid a relational wreck or help a searching soul. I don't like the feeling of meandering, but this may be God's way to protect me from my way. I am learning to appreciate the Lord's detours and not rush to my final destination. God's goal is not for me just to go from point A to point B. He longs for me to enjoy the journey.

Point to Ponder: Learn to appreciate the Lord's detours and not rush to the final destination.

Jesus followed His heavenly Father on a godly excursion. "So, [Jesus] left Judea and went back once more to Galilee. Now he had to go through Samaria" (John 4:3-4). Instead of hurrying back in an efficient pace to Galilee, He took His time to stop in Samaria to love a lady labeled unlovable by His culture. Jesus was intentional in instigating a relationship with a person who could not give Him anything in return. What seemed on the surface to be a less efficient schedule was more effective in God's kingdom. Jesus paused for one person. Giving the gift of eternal life to one individual trumped being expedient with many. He took a detour from the plan so He could follow the Father's plan.

Is your faith flexible? Can you joyfully follow your heavenly Father to places and people that are not a part of your original plan? Perhaps the Spirit is calling you to stay longer in your current circumstance so you can continue to model Jesus for those who have limited experience with Jesus. Maybe the Lord has detoured you to an unlit, uncrowded back road of life to test your belief and to grow your trust in Him. A life enamored by the noise and speed of busy highways can rush around only to discover Christ was just down the street in the cul-de-sac. Faith waits.

God's detours are opportunities to know others and to make God known. By faith, our uncertain and imperfect path leads us into the certainty of the Lord's perfect path. When His Spirit prompts our spirit to pause, we are wise to wait on His leading. Faith follows Jesus to people and places who need Jesus. His detours are His blessings in disguise. We are all blessed by impromptu love in Jesus's name. God's detours are the best route to enjoy His results. We should learn to pray with the psalmist, "Show me your ways, LORD, teach me your paths" (Psalm 25:4).

Heavenly Father, give me the courage to
change plans according to Your plans.

TAKEAWAY: *Relational leaders embrace divine detours.*

Summary of Chapter Seventeen Takeaways

1. Relational leaders look for divine appointments.
2. Relational leaders see the Lord working through life's interruptions.
3. Relational leaders embrace divine detours.

Chapter Eighteen

Invite Faith to Lead Feelings

*Teach me, LORD, the way of your decrees, that I may
follow it to the end. Give me understanding, so that I
may keep your law and obey it with all my heart.*

PSALM 119:33-34

*A thorough knowledge of the Bible is worth
more than a college education.*

THEODORE ROOSEVELT

Jesus Had Faith in and Obeyed Scripture Rather Than Flaky Feelings

Y ou have heard that it was said." These words begin one of the most significant reflections on the Old Testament that we find in the New Testament (see Matthew 5:21). Jesus uses this phrase to engage the teaching of the Hebrew Bible and applies it to the lives of His early disciples. The six examples given in Matthew 5 are commonly called "antitheses" and are the source of a common belief that Jesus "does away" with the old teaching of Judaism, replacing law with grace. "Jesus did away with all those stuffy rules and regulations," or so the argument goes. And yet, is that really what's going on here?

Rather than doing away with the law, in "fulfilling the law," I believe that Jesus is also extending the application of the law in new and radical ways, defining the nature of the church as a truly alternative form of society. Justice and goodness in the kingdom of God are not simply observing the minimum standard of the law but are instead meant to be the full embodiment of God's peace and self-giving love. This embodiment isn't just personal obedience to the law but is a vision of communal flourishing, living for the good of neighbor and community.

> **Point to Ponder:** *The law of God leads to grace for us to govern our feelings.*

Jesus wants us to be free from anger, not just for our own sake but so that we can live as citizens of a kingdom defined by reconciliation and love for others (see Matthew 5:21-26). He wants us to resist evil with non-violence so that we can model to the world an entirely new way of being, a way of being in which violence gives way to sacrificial love (5:38-42). And in troubled times like ours, when every day you and I seem to be forced to take sides, choosing whom we will love and whom we will hate, Jesus calls His people to embody the perfect love of heaven by seeing everyone we meet as beloved children of God, worthy of respect, affection, and dignity (5:43-48).

> **TAKEAWAY:** *Relational leaders align their feelings with the truth of Scripture.*

Feelings Tamed by Faith in God

I have a male friend in another state who has sexual feelings for men. Thankfully, years ago, he submitted his feelings to his faith in God to keep him from living out his inordinate desires. Once he gave over his feelings to his heavenly Father, his heavenly Father refused to give him over to his sinful desires. In essence, my friend took a different path than the people that Paul wrote about in Romans. "Therefore, God gave them over in the sinful desires of their hearts to sexual impurity for the degrading of their bodies with one another...In the same way the men also abandoned natural relations with women and were inflamed with lust for one another. Men committed shameful acts with other men, and received in themselves the due penalty for their error" (Romans 1:24-27). My friend's sexual feelings, harnessed by the Holy Spirit, kept him from a wild journey to find himself that he would one day regret. Desires need to be domesticated by God. The gospel is the power of God to protect us from our sinful desires. Faith tames our feelings.

Point to Ponder: *Desires need to be domesticated by God. The gospel is the power of God to protect us from our sinful desires.*

Paul outlines with clear logic and compelling love God's heart for those with distorted affections. Generally speaking, the Lord protects us from ourselves, unless we demand to act on our sinful desires. Paul could have been addressing a contemporary audience when he described a group who exchanged the truth about God for a lie. That truth might have been "God loves us," while the lie might have been that "He will allow us to exchange natural sexual relations for unnatural ones: women inflamed with lust for other women and men inflamed with lust for other men." Because of their rebellion—like prodigal children—God gave them over to the sinful desires of their hearts, degrading their bodies with one another. "It is God's will that you should be sanctified: that you should avoid sexual immorality; that each of you should learn to control your own body in a way that is holy and honorable, not in passionate lust like the pagans, who do not know God" (1 Thessalonians 4:3-5).

Are your feelings submitted to your faith in God? Grace is not a "get out of jail free card" to act out inordinate affections. Sinful desires like greed, anger, selfishness, sexual lust, and pride need the governor of God's grace to protect you from yourself. Trust in the Lord is able to tame your feelings over time. Perhaps when you don't get your way, you are able to see anger coming. Instead of getting mad at another who does seem to get their way, simply trust Christ will have His way in the long run. When lust disguises itself as love, expose its hypocrisy and have faith to wait on God's best. Feelings must be led by faith in Jesus.

How do we love well those being led astray by their untamed feelings? We lovingly lead them back to the truth of God—discovered and understood by their faith in God. Yes, it is a relational risk to remind someone we love that their heavenly Father's greater love does not condone affections that conflict with His holiness and compete with His purity plan for His creation. Prayerfully administer truth as a serum to restore a soul to its senses. Faith tames feelings. Follow Paul's bold proclamation of truth: "For I am not ashamed of the gospel, because it is the power of God that brings salvation to everyone who believes: first to the Jew, then to the Gentile. For in the gospel the righteousness of God is revealed—a righteousness that is by faith from first to last, just as it is written: 'The righteous will live by faith'" (Romans 1:16-17).

Heavenly Father, harness my desires by Your
grace, love, and wisdom. In Jesus's name, amen.

TAKEAWAY: *Relational leaders seek to administer truth as a serum so that errant feelings submit to faith.*

Feelings Are Wonderful Servants but Terrible Masters

The Corinthian Christians embraced Paul's message of freedom in Christ with great zeal and excitement. Rather than living under the weight of the law, with its demands and moral restraints, they now had a way to follow God and still indulge freely in the sexually indulgent society in which they lived. In short, they said, "If Jesus came to set us free, surely that freedom means we are now liberated to do the things we want to do, to give in to any desire that we may feel." Paul responded this way: "All things are lawful for me, but I will not be dominated by anything. For you were bought with a price; therefore, glorify God in your body" (1 Corinthians 6:12b, 20 NRSV).

As J.P. Moreland says, "Feelings are wonderful servants but terrible masters." God does not want you to shut down your emotions and desires, but He does want them to be used to propel your life into an ever-increasing alignment with His kingdom. Paul isn't condemning the fact that they deeply desire something, he's warning them against being mastered by a desire that is out of step with God's best for them.

Sexual desire is one of the deepest and strongest longings known to humankind. It is so powerful that, before we even realize it, we can find ourselves enslaved to its demands. Sexual slavery promises release while always deepening its hold. It is never content to leave you as you are but will relentlessly push you deeper into dark places, places you never thought you would go. What starts as "innocent" flirtation with a colleague grows into a deep emotional attachment that becomes a full-blown affair. An unguarded embrace of our culture's incessant objectification of women enslaves us to the cheap, self-serving gratification found in pornography and the strip club.

God wants you to master your desires before they master you. He deeply desires that you know, embody, and walk in the freedom won for you through the self-giving love of Jesus. In Paul's language, we "glorify God in our bodies" when we live as free women and free men. That does not mean free to indulge every desire, but free to subject those desires to an even greater longing to know the abundant life of God.

The Lord invites you to walk in His ways not because He wants to keep you from your desires, but because He knows our desires can be broken and misleading. The courage we need to align our desires with God's values is rooted in the belief that His will is for our good and ultimate flourishing. As Paul reminds us elsewhere, "For freedom Christ has set us free. Stand firm, therefore, and do not submit again to a yoke of slavery" (Galatians 5:1). Where do your desires dominate you and keep you enslaved?

Father, in Your love, free us from the slavery
of sexual sin and redirect our desires toward
You, through Christ our Lord. Amen.

TAKEAWAY: *Relational leaders recognize feelings as helpful servants and refuse to let them become harsh masters.*

Summary of Chapter Eighteen Takeaways

1. Relational leaders align their feelings with the truth of Scripture.

2. Relational leaders seek to administer truth as a serum so that errant feelings submit to faith.

3. Relational leaders recognize feelings as helpful servants and refuse to let them become harsh masters.

Chapter Nineteen

Pray for and with Others

*For this reason I kneel before the Father, from whom
every family in heaven and on earth derives its name. I
pray that out of his glorious riches he may strengthen you
with power through His Spirit in your inner being, so
that Christ may dwell in your hearts through faith.*

EPHESIANS 3:14-17

*Our prayers may be awkward. Our attempts may be feeble.
But since the power of prayer is in the one who hears it and
not in the one who says it, our prayers do make a difference.*

MAX LUCADO

Jesus Taught Us How to Pray

One day Jesus was praying in a certain place. When he finished, one of his disciples said to him, 'Lord, teach us to pray, just as John taught his disciples.' He said to them, 'When you pray, say: Father, hallowed be your name, your kingdom come'" (Luke 11:1-2). This prayer of Jesus, otherwise known as the Lord's prayer, is our model for prayer. Jesus, characteristically, created consistent time to be with His heavenly Father. One day, upon conclusion of His private prayers, a perceptive disciple asked Jesus for prayer instruction for himself and the other disciples. His response, this prayer, was birthed out of Jesus's intimacy with His heavenly Father. He could instruct them on prayer with authority because He prayed with authority.

Point to Ponder: *The reverent and submissive spirit of our Lord's prayer is the navigator for our prayers.*

The significance of the Lord's Prayer is as much the spirit of the prayer as it is the words of the prayer. The Lord spoke about prayer after He had just prayed. Only minutes before, He had bowed in humble worship, seeking the face of His heavenly Father. He gloried in the One who sent Him from heaven to earth to save the world. Oh, what a privilege to pray in the presence of our all-wise God. Our spirits, expunged of all selfish pride, are replenished with selfless humility. The reverent and submissive spirit of our Lord's prayer is the navigator of our prayers.

When in Doubt, Pray

"The spirit is willing, but the flesh is weak" (Matthew 26:41). Our flesh seeks to dismiss the power of prayer by questioning its effectiveness: "Does it really matter if I pray or not?" "Are things truly any different after I pray than before I pray?" In His prayer, Jesus desires all men and women everywhere to pray with hands lifted high in praise and hearts bowed low in protracted submission. Jesus is heavenly minded and has earthly aspirations. He prays for God's kingdom to be ushered onto earth with the splendor of heaven's resources. He prays for our globe to be governed by God, for God, and with God. The prayer of Jesus pronounces God king!

The prayer of Jesus is our model of how and what to pray. Begin and end with Him. Satan shrinks back at the supplications set forth by our Savior. Therefore, we take His instructions to heart. These words are not a magical chant, but a divine mandate to seek the love of our heavenly Father, fear His holiness, align with His will, ask His provision, receive His forgiveness, trust His power, and announce His glory. Pray His prayer as your prayer!

Heavenly Father, help me make the prayer
of Jesus my pattern for prayer.

TAKEAWAY: *The prayer of Jesus is a good model for relational leaders to pray.*

Relational Leaders Pray Selfless Prayers

My friend Jim was CEO over a large private company for 15 years. His employees loved him because he loved them. One way he expressed his care was convening every Monday for voluntary prayer of all faiths. Over the span of 15 minutes, he would facilitate an opportunity for team members to share prayer needs, from daunting health issues for themselves and loved ones to more global problems. Each person respected the others' faith. No one ever complained of being prayed for—the company's culture encouraged prayer.

Friends snared by sin need our prayers, not our prognosis. God's portion is to convict and change lives; our part is prayer. There is definitely a time and place to confront a believer in disobedience. However, we are not the judge—God is. Others-centered praying is freeing for both the person praying and the person for whom the prayer is being prayed. As we pray for others, we are freed from preoccupation with our own problems. "And the Lord accepted Job's prayer. After Job had prayed for his friends, the Lord made him prosperous again and gave him twice as much as he had before" (Job 42:9-10).

> **Point to Ponder:** As we pray for others, we are freed from preoccupation with our own problems.

Prayer Is an Expression of Love for Others

The severity of another's needs tends to dwarf our own. The posture of prayer for another renders our perspectives healthier. Our gratitude grows through selfless prayer. We learn to count our many blessings and be content. Of course, it is okay to ask God's favor on our life, but not at the expense of excluding prayer for others. Isaac offers a model of intercession: "Isaac prayed to the LORD on behalf of his wife, because she was barren. The LORD answered his prayer, and his wife Rebekah became pregnant" (Genesis 25:21).

Authentic Christianity results in love for people. Is prayer a meaningful way to love? Of course, and the greatest test may be to pray for those who do not pray for you. This is truly unselfish praying. Your only reward may be a clear conscience before God. Pray for your adversaries and trust the Lord to accomplish His purpose in their life in His time. As Jesus said, "Love your enemies and pray for those who persecute you" (Matthew 5:44).

An exciting part of praying for others is the change you experience. Prayer for people cultivates an attitude of love and forgiveness in the person praying that no human counselor can provide. Godly counsel can guide you there, but only God can produce the transformation of the heart. Prayer places you face to face with your heavenly Father so that you can recognize your need for forgiveness.

Most importantly, pray for those outside of faith in Christ. Paul gives us an example: "Brothers and sisters, my heart's desire and prayer to God for the Israelites is that they may be saved" (Romans 10:1). You can pray boldly, knowing that their salvation is God's will. Pray that God will use you, circumstances, and other believers to draw others to Him. A stubborn heart is no match for prayer. Satan's deception is no match for prayer. Prayer can travel behind enemy lines and accomplish more in a moment than a lifetime of worry and work. Pray for sinners to be saved and glorify God.

Heavenly Father, grow my heart to intersect with those in
need of healing in body and soul. In Jesus's name, amen.

TAKEAWAY: *Relational leaders pray selfless prayers.*

Relational Leaders Are Thankful for Answered Prayer

"Then Jesus looked up and said, 'Father, I thank you that you have heard me. I knew that you always hear me, but I said this for the benefit of the people standing here, that they may believe that you sent me'" (John 11:41-42). Jesus thanked His Father for answered prayer—even before His prayer was answered! His heart was so in tune with the heart of the Father that He could boldly ask, knowing it was the will of God. In the same way, our Savior calls us to align our hearts with our heavenly Father's heart. His plan is for our desires to be His desires, our wants to be His wants, our goals to be His goals, our will to be His will, and our prayers to be His prayers. Hence, we can thank Him for answered prayers!

What prayers are yet to be answered, but need to be prayed? What is Christ asking you to confidently pray in His name, knowing that He will answer in the future? Perhaps it's a yet-to-be determined job promotion that you can thank God for now. You can praise the Lord today for your wayward child, about whom you have a peace in your heart that they will eventually come back to their Savior Jesus. Or, you pray with the Spirit's certainty over an uncertain illness that threatens your joy. You can face whatever you have to with faith in your heavenly Father who hears your prayer. "You may ask me for anything in my name, and I will do it" (John 14:14).

> **Point to Ponder:** *You can face whatever you have to with faith in your heavenly Father who hears your prayer.*

Becoming an Answer to Our Prayers

We ask in Jesus's name when we pray for Him to be glorified through answered prayer. When Jesus is lifted up, all men and women are drawn to Him. We ask in Christ's name when our desire is for our answered prayers to be a benefit for believers to grow in their faith and for unbelievers to come to faith. Oh the joy of seeing someone come to know Jesus in personal salvation because they saw the love of God transform the life of a loved one!

As we look to the Lord and thank Him for answered prayer, He may call us to be a part of His provision. Jesus told the disciples to pray to the Lord of the harvest for laborers, and as they prayed, He called them to labor for Him. So, what is your role in relation to the future prayers He wants to answer on your behalf? Perhaps you can meet the need or call on someone else that can provide answers. Be grateful, for God has you positioned to be a part of His answered prayers!

Talk with Jesus often about the needs of others, but be careful; you may become an answer to your own prayer. Pray for a friend in financial need, and the Lord may lead you to assist. Pray for a relative whose heart is hard, and God may lead you to soften this person with kindness. Pray for a child who has lost a parent, and you may become his or her parent. Pray for the leadership needs at the church, and by faith you may step into that leadership role. Be keenly aware of what you pray, as you may become the answer to your own prayer. "Then [Jesus] said to them, 'The harvest truly is great, but the laborers are few; therefore pray the Lord of the harvest to send out laborers into His harvest'" (Luke 10:2 NKJV).

Heavenly Father, I praise You for the assurance
of answered prayers in the future.

TAKEAWAY: *Sometimes relational leaders become an answer to their own prayers.*

Praying for and with others is a compelling way to show compassion. I like how Henri Nouwen describes this process as the regular reflection of a loving heart: "Prayer for others, therefore, cannot be seen as an extraordinary exercise that must be practiced from time to time. Rather, it is the very beat of the compassionate heart."[2]

Summary of Chapter Nineteen Takeaways

1. The prayer of Jesus is a good model for relational leaders to pray.

2. Relational leaders pray selfless prayers.

3. Sometimes relational leaders become an answer to their own prayers.

Chapter Twenty

Grow a Generous Life

You will be enriched in every way so that you can
be generous on every occasion, and through us your
generosity will result in thanksgiving to God.

2 CORINTHIANS 9:11

People will forget what you said, and people will forget what
you did, but people will never forget how you made them feel.

MAYA ANGELO

Jesus Was Generous with God's Graces

Christmas day is always an exercise in expectancy of giving and receiving gifts. I marvel at the joy of our children and grandchildren, as their beautifully wrapped boxes and packages become tangled ribbons and wrinkled wrapping paper. What gives me the most pause is their genuine gratitude to one another for their gifts. I thank the Lord for putting in their hearts and minds a spirit of true thankfulness (and their parents for reminding them!). I also pray for all of us who are maturing in the faith to grow more and more grateful for God's blessings. An abundant Christian life is a life ever-growing in God's graces.

> **Point to Ponder:** An abundant Christian life is a life ever-growing in God's graces.

Jude, brother of James and the half-brother of Jesus, experienced first-hand the mercy, peace, and love of Christ ("May God give you more and more mercy, peace, and love" [Jude 1:2 NLT]). Jude probably saw Jesus show mercy to the woman caught in adultery who was forgiven and instructed to sin no more. Perhaps Jude was one of the disciples who, after resurrection, was in the presence of the Lord when He breathed the Spirit on them and said, "Peace be with you." Christ poured out His love on those poor in spirit—He fed, He healed, He taught, He suffered, He died, He rose from the dead—all for the sake of His vast love.

Relational Leaders Reciprocate Generosity in God's Graces

Does your spiritual balance sheet show an excess in God's graces? Are your line items of mercy, peace, and love under or over budget? Those who are rich in the true riches of Christ show mercy to the deviant, though they are careful not to condone the sin. Those who grow more and more in peace are calm, because they have learned to submit to the rule of Christ's peace over their hearts. Their softened face exudes love, their kind words communicate love, and their supportive actions express love. Why? Because vibrant relational leaders continue to grow more and more in God's graces.

As we learn to receive more and more from our heavenly Father—His mercy, peace, and love—we are able to give more and more mercy, peace, and love. Generosity born from an awareness of God's grace is the greatest generosity. Generosity expresses itself in aggressive giving. Next time we are offended, we can immediately show mercy and not allow hurt to have its way in our heart. When fear threatens to derail us, we can remain calm by looking into the peaceful eyes of Jesus. When we are loved well, we can love well. "Grow in the grace and knowledge of our Lord and Savior Jesus Christ. To him be glory both now and forever! Amen" (2 Peter 3:18).

Heavenly Father, I receive Your mercy, peace, and love, so I can abundantly give Your mercy, peace, and love.

TAKEAWAY: *Relational leaders generously show grace because of the grace they have been shown.*

Relational Leaders Practice Generous Parenting

I admire Cindy Jones-Nyland's generous service during her teenage years, which was inspired by her mom:

> I remember as a young girl (age 12), my mom volunteered me to take care of an elderly lady in our community. She was a fixture in the community, the pillar of one of the families in our small town of less than 200. Ms. Angie wanted to live at home and not be forced to live part of her elderly life in an assisted living facility. But she was not able to do all of the things that allowed her freedom. However, with a little help, she was able to live independently and with a deep sense of pride.
>
> I was "volunteered" to spend my mornings and evenings with her on most days. It meant that she could spend the rest of the time free to be at home. I didn't know what to think at first. This meant that early mornings before school and late evenings after sports were spent helping care for her from the time I was 12 until I left for college at 18. (I ended up getting paid for my time–financially, spiritually, and emotionally). I know it changed my life. I got as much out of that amazing experience as Angie did. And I know we will be forever connected in ways I still feel today.[3]

"The righteous gives and does not hold back" (Proverbs 21:26 ESV).

More Blessed to Give Than Receive

As parents, we love to give good gifts to our children. In fact, I think we find more joy in giving than our kids do in receiving! I want to encourage you to give your kids an intentional gift: help them understand that it does bring more fulfillment and joy to give than to receive. It is so easy for our children to think that the entire world exists for their desires, wants, and needs. Yet Jesus reminds us "it is more blessed to give than to receive" (Acts 20:35).

Even our children can offer gifts to the glory of God and for the life of the world. If this sounds great as a concept, but you're clueless on how to begin to take steps in this direction, fear not! You're certainly not alone. To grow in this lifestyle of gratitude and generosity, we parents must be intentional. Generosity and gratitude must be nurtured and sought out in our lives.

> **Point to Ponder:** Even our children can offer gifts to the glory of God and for the life of the world.

Generous living isn't a default mode but a purposeful decision. If you'd like to buy a gift for a family in need, put a shopping trip on your calendar right now. Look up service opportunities in your community and find a time to serve those in need as a family. And if you've never talked to your kids about the countless ways that money can be a blessing to others, then take time over dinner this week to do so. Small but intentional steps in the right direction can lead to significant growth over time.

When we as parents prioritize this way of life, our kids see its importance. In the midst of the busyness of life, let us be intentional with how we use our time and look for creative ways to lead our families into deeper and richer lives of faithful and generous living.

Heavenly Father, may we respond to Your great love for us by giving freely of ourselves so that we can be a gift to others.

> **TAKEAWAY:** Relational leaders practice generous parenting.

Relational Leaders Are Generous Toward God

The God of the universe looks for those who would be with Him. The psalmist captures perfectly the spirit that God desires: "You, God, are my God, earnestly I seek you; I thirst for you, my whole being longs for you, in a dry and parched land where there is no water. I have seen you in the sanctuary and beheld your power and your glory. Because your love is better than life, my lips will glorify you" (Psalm 63:1-3). The Lord longs for His children to take time to experience His tender, loving presence. Almighty God is not needy, but He wants His creation to come before Him in humble dependence. He knows that prayer is what's best for those He bought with His Son's blood. Being generous toward God through daily doses of solitude and communion is the wisest gift we can give to God. Our presence gratifies God.

> **Point to Ponder:** *Being generous toward God through daily doses of solitude and communion is the wisest gift we can give to God.*

Like an earthly father revels in the joy of being close to his precious child, so our heavenly Father smiles to see us—His children—sit next to Him. The grace of God is not experienced without parking our lives in His presence, turning off the engine of our activity, and activating His perspective in our heart and mind. We invest in intimacy with our heavenly Father in order to fulfill His agenda in our daily calendar.

Time Invested with God Is Time Well Spent

Be careful not to slip into a routine of perfunctory prayers that miss the heart of your master. Engage with Christ so that He can help you to better understand His heart and embrace His way. Time with Him can take a variety of forms. Maybe you commune with Christ as you walk alone in a solemn cathedral, or perhaps you celebrate Jesus in raucous worship with other Christ followers at Sunday church services. You may engage Him as you stroll in your neighborhood, sit by a quiet fire, rest by a bubbling creek, or watch His heavenly handiwork in a brilliant sunrise or sunset. Above all else, be still, know that He is God, be loved by Him, and then love on His behalf. He says, "Be still, and know that I am God; I will be exalted among the nations, I will be exalted in the earth" (Psalm 46:10). Time with the Lord is never wasted.

*Heavenly Father, I long to give You my time, to
be loved by You, and to love others.*

TAKEAWAY: *Relational leaders are generous toward Jesus with their time and reap benefits as a result.*

Summary of Chapter Twenty Takeaways

1. Relational leaders generously show grace because of the grace they have been shown.
2. Relational leaders practice generous parenting.
3. Relational leaders are generous toward Jesus with their time and reap benefits as a result.

Chapter Twenty-One

Model What You Expect

*I became your father through the gospel. Therefore I urge you
to imitate me. For this reason I have sent to you Timothy,
my son whom I love, who is faithful in the Lord. He
will remind you of my way of life in Christ Jesus, which
agrees with what I teach everywhere in every church.*

1 CORINTHIANS 4:15-17

*Children also catch a lot by way of example. If parents are
disrespectful, children will catch it like a cold. If parents are
gracious, children will bask in it like the beach on a sunny day.*

MICHAEL CANNON LOEHRER

Jesus Was the Best Example

Jesus gave them this answer: "Very truly I tell you, the Son can do nothing by himself; he can do only what he sees his Father doing, because whatever the Father does the Son also does" (John 5:19). Jesus followed the example of His heavenly Father. He only did what His Father did. In the same way, we who love Christ seek to follow His example. In the power of the Holy Spirit, we can do what He does. We can do nothing of eternal significance in our own strength, but in His strength we can do His works. Thus, we start with Jesus when we initiate new activities. We ask Him to validate our direction before we move forward. We want to follow His wise example.

Point to Ponder: We can do nothing of eternal significance in our own strength, but in Christ's strength we can do His works.

Jesus put individual needs before the needs of institutions. He did not allow religious leaders to keep Him from doing good for those who suffered under bad circumstances. "Now if a boy can be circumcised on the Sabbath so that the law of Moses may not be broken, why are you angry with me for healing a man's whole body on the Sabbath" (John 7:23)? The Sabbath was holy to God, but it was also an opportunity to glorify God by curing those in physical pain. The mercy and compassion of Christ trumps the unnecessary sacrifice required by some religious leaders' strict rules. Relationships take priority over rules.

Follow Good Examples

Follow the examples of those who follow Christ well, especially in their humility in pointing people back to Jesus. They are quick to say that anything worth emulating in their lives comes from the life of Christ in them. Their goal is for others to fall deeper in love with their heavenly Father and to only do what He leads them to do. They seek to observe the life of Christ and His Word—the Bible. Good role models point people to the Lord.

As Paul told Timothy, "Set an example for the believers in speech, in conduct, in love, in faith, and in purity" (1 Timothy 4:12). When you hurt a child's feelings, ask their forgiveness. When you pray, humbly confess your sins before you pray for the needs of others. When you worship God, focus on His glory and goodness. When you give, give discreetly and generously. When you serve, don't expect to be served. Use your freedom in Christ to do what's wise, not just what's permissible. Be a good example who follows the example of Jesus. Many who respect you may model what you do.

Heavenly Father, I desire to be a good example
that follows Your example, and I want to be
a good example for others to follow.

TAKEAWAY: *Relational leaders follow the examples of those who follow Christ well.*

Relational Leaders Seek to Leave a Legacy for Christ

Recently, I came home to a sad sight. Our six-year-old grandson, Hudson, with sullen face, said slowly, almost weeping, "Pop, we can't have pizza tonight." My wife, Rita, affectionately known as Bibi (Swahili for "grandmother"), explained the broader context, "I have hamburger patties prepared to grill tonight and tomorrow for dinner we will enjoy pizza." I thought about telling my little man to suck it up and change his attitude, but instead I thought, *Let's make this a fun, teachable moment for all of us.* So, I knelt down, looked my disheartened grandson in the eyes, and attempted to turn this into a helpful, enjoyable life lesson.

"Sometimes in life, we don't get our way, and even though we are disappointed we can have a grateful attitude for all we do have. So, Hudson, we are going to play a game called the Gratitude Game, and you are in charge of keeping score. Every time Bibi or I catch you or one of your two brothers being thankful, you receive a point." "Thank you, Pop, for putting me in charge." "Hudson, you just earned a point!" For the next 24 hours, three motivated grandsons looked for ways to be grateful. The two oldest, not surprisingly, tied with 38 points, and the youngest scored a respectable 13 points. All contestants celebrated with a $5 award to spend at the dollar store!

> **Point to Ponder:** Faith in Christ is the best gift a grand-parent can give a grandchild.

The Best Gift

"I am reminded of your sincere faith, which first lived in your grand-mother Lois and in your mother Eunice and, I am persuaded, now lives in you also" (2 Timothy 1:5). A legacy of faith in Christ was the best gift Timothy's mom and grandmother could give him; sadly, his dad was still an unbeliever (Acts 16:1). What he learned as a child was embraced as his own faith as an adult. His mentor, Paul, saw compelling evidence of a faith alive in the heart of his protégé. No doubt Timothy lived out what he saw first-hand from the hands of his faithful mom and grand-mother: perhaps hands that tucked him in at night with reassuring prayers, hands that comforted his hurting heart, or hands that prepared him meals. Grandparents have a captive audience in the grandchildren who are open to learn about God and watch faith in action.

Being an engaged grandparent can be exhausting, so we are wise to pace ourselves and not allow our fatigue to force us to forget the bigger purpose of being in the life of our little ones: to be an attractive example of what it means to love and follow Jesus. Don't look for the perfect situation to speak truth; in fact, it's sometimes better for a child to learn life lessons from their very real and imperfect world. Take the time to pray together for those suffering from a natural disaster and show them how to give directly to those in need. Or, greet the trash collectors with a $20 tip and thank them for their helpful service. Look for ways to give.

We seek to teach our grandchildren about genuine faith in God through Jesus Christ. Read them the Bible stories of Hannah's prayers, David's courage, Ruth's love, Joseph's forgiveness, and Jesus's humility. Take them to church, explain what it means to become a Christian and why baptism is important. Tell them stories of other faithful Christians like Corrie ten Boom, William Wilberforce, Henrietta Mears, and Bill Bright. Christianity is caught as well as taught, so be a contagious Christian and infect your grandchild with a heart of intimacy for their Savior Jesus and a heart of integrity for their friends. Look for teachable moments and teach! "Start children off on the way they should go, and even when they are old they will not turn from it" (Proverbs 22:6).

Heavenly Father, help me to show my grandchildren
Your wise ways. In Jesus's name, amen.

TAKEAWAY: *Relational leaders seek to leave a legacy for Christ.*

Relational Leaders Model the Way with Their Attitude, Actions, and Words

"I have set you an example that you should do as I have done for you" (John 13:15). We start by modeling our attitude. Attitude is everything. It is the difference between goodness and greatness. It separates the mature from the immature. Attitude is what causes people to give up or persevere. The leader has a responsibility to inspire hope with an optimistic attitude. Anyone can be negative and assign blame, but wise is the leader who is positive and takes responsibility. This is the attitude God blesses. He dispenses more opportunity to one whose attitude is aligned with His agenda. The attitude God honors is humble, unselfish, and hopeful in Him.

Proper attitude alignment requires a prayerful attitude. This attitude depends on God and seeks His wisdom. It is a positive attitude that always looks for the good in an individual or situation. A prayerful attitude is also an appreciative attitude. Gratitude generates a right attitude because it rarely complains. Our attitude is infectious and our actions speak volumes. It is imperative that we model attractive actions. Behavior validates our beliefs. If we say one thing and do another, we are dishonest with others and ourselves. Actions are a measure of our character. Appropriate actions earn us the right to influence and lead. If we are inconsistent in our actions, we confuse the team. Consistent actions facilitate faithfulness in followers.

> **Point to Ponder:** *Proper attitude alignment requires a prayerful attitude.*

The Bible Is Our Baseline for Behavior

The manner in which we arrive at our definition of right actions is important. Work expectations are based on the principles found in God's Word. The Bible is our baseline for behavior. Good leaders illustrate respectful behavior and reinforce it with collaborative discussions. Wise actions then become the norm for an effective and efficient work culture. Wise actions are marked by follow-through. We do what we say and say what we do. A wise leader also solicits feedback from everyone. We rely on the wisdom of the team over our own perspective. The Bible defines right actions, so while everyone on the team may not believe in Jesus, they all agree to act like Jesus when they agree to do the right thing.

Lastly, you model with your words. Words can build up or tear down. Your words can be pure and encouraging or poisonous and discouraging. Moment by moment, you have the opportunity to inject courage into your colleagues with truthful, kind, and caring words. Measure your words prayerfully and patiently before you speak. Do not allow anger and harshness to dominate your delivery. Use words as an ointment rather than an irritant. Your words are a reflection of your heart. A healed heart produces healing words. Therefore, use words wisely by speaking as you would like to be spoken to—with a spirit of compassion. When you speak, build up rather than tear down. Speak the truth in love. Choose caring conflict over insensitive passive aggressiveness. Words matter, so model your speech well. Above all else, model the way by following Jesus's way. As He stated, "I am the way and the truth and the life" (John 14:6a).

Heavenly Father, I look to Your son Jesus as my example for life, so others can be inspired by my life.

TAKEAWAY: *Relational leaders model the way with their attitude, actions, and words.*

Summary of Chapter Twenty-One Takeaways

1. Relational leaders follow the examples of those who follow Christ well.

2. Relational leaders seek to leave a legacy for Christ.

3. Relational leaders model the way with their attitude, actions, and words.

Chapter Twenty-Two

Anticipate Where God Is at Work

Brothers and sisters, I do not consider myself yet to have taken hold of it. But one thing I do: Forgetting what is behind and straining toward what is ahead, I press on toward the goal to win the prize for which God has called me heavenward in Christ Jesus. All of us, then, who are mature should take such a view of things. And if on some point you think differently, that too God will make clear to you.

PHILIPPIANS 3:13-15

Never forget that anticipation is an important part of life. Work's important, family's important, but without excitement, you have nothing. You're cheating yourself if you refuse to enjoy what's coming.

NICHOLAS SPARKS

Jesus Anticipated Finishing His Assignment

I have brought you glory on earth by finishing the work you gave me to do" (John 17:4). Godly ambition brings glory to God. Yet, I don't always reflect the glory back to my heavenly Father. My motives become mixed. I want to be thought of in a good light and given credit for my accomplishments. But, the Holy Spirit reminds me that my Savior Jesus needs to be in the spotlight, not me. He is the light of all men; I am only an illumination of His greater glory. Any industry success is an illustration of the Spirit at work through my work. I am learning to die to my drive for success and instead follow God. Godly ambition leads us to deflect credit away from ourselves.

Jesus finished the work assignment given to Him by His heavenly

Father. Satan's hellish agenda could not lure the Lord Christ away from His heavenly mission. Suffering did not give Jesus an excuse to exchange His pain for a renouncement of His equality with Almighty God. Instead, He surrendered His desires and submitted to the will of His Father. At His death, the ungodly ambitions of sinful men were nailed to the cross. To quote Hebrews, we must "consider him who endured such opposition from sinners, so that you will not grow weary and lose heart" (Hebrews 12:3).

The path of godly ambition is not without resistance or rejection. Those with competing agendas may very well oppose our Spirit-led agendas. Some may try to discredit our work so that they get credit for the work. If so, we trust the Lord to bring honor to Himself; we do not have to highjack the process. Godly ambition waits on the Holy Spirit to work in spite of unholy influences. When we stay focused on being faithful to our calling, God does His work!

Godly ambition leads us to finish the work of God. As Paul puts it, "I press on toward the goal to win the prize for which God has called me heavenward in Christ Jesus" (Philippians 3:14). Thoroughness is an attribute of those who trust in the Lord to use their gifts and skills for His glory. We stay on point so we can point people to Christ. Furthermore, we adjust along the way to meet the needs of those who need us. We may say no to an opportunity so we have more time to invest in a needy individual. Godly ambition trusts God. We get less attention so we are available to give attention to other needy souls. Ultimately, we die to ourselves so Christ can live through us.

*Heavenly Father, give me a heart of selfless
ambition that glorifies You in the process.*

Relational Leaders Are Hopeful for a Better Future

"Pop, this is my favorite." These are precious, never to be forgotten words from my 4-year-old grandson after we witnessed our favorite college football players walk ten feet in front of us into their locker room. It felt surreal as I shared that experience with my son-in-law and two grandsons. I cherished the moment. I lifted my moist eyes upward to whisper a "thank you" to my heavenly Father, grateful to feel the connection of a special moment with my family. I was ambushed by joy!

Point to Ponder: Shared joy makes life twice as good and half as hard.

Later, I asked myself, "What was the big deal?" While processing my emotions, I realized that I had a longing to be with my grandsons and son-in-law and experience a bigger-than-life event. I was reminded of a quote from a friend's father who had enjoyed a similar occasion with his son and grandsons—"Sometimes we don't have to have dreams for dreams to come true." This rang true for me. I didn't realize how much this brief moment in my life would bring to light my heart's desire. This experience of joy shared with those who loved me the most was a life-giving grace to my soul. As the proverb goes, "A longing fulfilled is sweet to the soul" (Proverbs 13:19).

What dream sits dormant in your soul? Are you unaware of a deep desire that patiently waits to ambush you with joy? Or perhaps there is a deferred hope you are trusting the Lord to fulfill. Whatever your situation, be encouraged that your heavenly Father specializes in making dreams come true, even those of which you are unaware. Perhaps you have not verbalized your desire for fear of setting expectations too high and being let down. Confront your fear and command it to stand down, for love is your weapon to defeat the enemy of reluctance that threatens your soul. Joy awaits you.

Do you hope and pray one day for your child or your parent to seek a relationship with you? Don't give up! Pray. Keep initiating conversations, sending texts, and sharing photos. Your seeds of sincere love hopefully will fall on good soil in God's timing. Trust Him to unite you. Maybe you feel your career is a dead-end road; if so, seek the Lord's off ramps to other opportunities. Perhaps reinvent yourself with a new skill set that opens new doors to serve. Your dream may be dead or at best illusive, but stay hopeful and trust Jesus that one day, when you least expect it, He will ambush you with joy. "I remain confident of this: I will see the goodness of the LORD in the land of the living. Wait for the LORD; be strong and take heart and wait for the LORD" (Psalm 27:13-14).

> *Heavenly Father, I celebrate and thank You*
> *for the unexpected joyful occasions that fill our*
> *hearts and souls with thanksgiving and praise*
> *for Your goodness. In Jesus's name, amen.*

TAKEAWAY: *Relational leaders hope for a better future.*

Dream Big Dreams

I heard a sound bite of an emotional and grateful Dabo Swinney (Clemson head football coach) from his first press conference. "I want to tell everyone to dream big and believe, because dreams come true, and today I am very humbled that one of my dreams has come true." Growing up in adversity, Dabo learned that hard work motivated by character resulted in good outcomes. Many say he has built the best culture in college football to influence and equip young men for lifetime achievement. I believe God wants us to trust Him with our big dreams.

Point to Ponder: God wants us to trust Him with our big dreams.

Representing an oppressed people, the prophet Habakkuk looks to the Lord for His vision of what's to come.

> The Lord said to me, "Write my answer on a billboard, large and clear, so that anyone can read it at a glance and rush to tell the others. But these things I plan won't happen right away. Slowly, steadily, surely, the time approaches when the vision will be fulfilled. If it seems slow, do not despair, for these things will surely come to pass. Just be

patient! They will not be overdue a single day!" (Habakkuk 2:2-3 TLB).

Will people we know and love be set free from abomination and injustice? If so, when? What is God's vision for His people? Habakkuk did his part to "stand at his watch" in defense of his people. In solitude, in stillness, high above on the ramparts he prayed and looked to the Lord for a divine vision of what was to come. Through silence, "his doing" was devoured by the divine and "his being" was ready to receive the vision. The Lord instructed him to write down words delivered by the Spirit to his conscience and his soul soaked it up. Linger and wait on God's timing. "Whatever you do, do it as service to Him, and *He* will guarantee your success" (Proverbs 16:3 THE VOICE).

What Big Dream Is in Your Heart?

What big dream is in your heart? Perhaps it is the dream of one day having a family—a family who loves each other, who enjoys each other's company so much they can't wait to be together. Perhaps it is the dream of a work culture where everyone works hard for a compelling purpose so that they serve one another above themselves—a place of employment where you can't wait to get to work. Perhaps you dream of a life full not of drama and pain, but of stability and healing. Perhaps you dream of relationships that are growing and fulfilling, a community of like-minded friends who really know one another and still cherish and love one another. Dream big dreams; trust God for their reality.

Linger with the Lord as you wait for Him to do His work in and through you. Allow your doing to be devoured by God's love, so your being can be fully loved by Him. Out of your place of peace and contentment Christ will take you to the places you need to go. Confusion may seem to be in charge, but you can trust Jesus to have the last word and to use bad circumstances to accomplish good things. Write down what the Spirit is saying to your soul. Documenting that is risky, because you may fail, but it is better to fail by faith than not to do anything because of fear. The just live by faith. Dream big dreams with your big God and watch Him do big things. Slowly, steadily, God will work! "Be delighted with the Lord. Then he will give you all your heart's desires" (Psalm 37:4 TLB).

> *Heavenly Father, by faith I trust You to align my desires*
> *with Your desires and for You to give me the desires of*
> *my heart for Your glory. In Jesus's name I pray, amen.*

TAKEAWAY: Relational leaders anticipate where God is at work and join Him.

Relational Leaders Anticipate God's Gifts

Anticipation or looking forward to something good is a highlight of life. I like to anticipate good food and seeing family over the Christmas season. I take advantage of a break from work. My mind feasts on a good book and my body rests from a rigorous routine. I look forward to college football. Also, I take satisfaction in knowing that the children and grandchildren will enjoy each other. Watching them rip open neatly wrapped gifts brings great joy to my wife and me. But most importantly, I anticipate the celebration of God's gift, the birth of His Son—Jesus.

Point to Ponder: Linger with the Lord as you wait for Him to do His work in and through you.

The men from the East were wise to anticipate the arrival of the King of the Jews—Jesus.

> Wise men from the East came to Jerusalem, saying, "Where is He who has been born King of the Jews? For we have seen His star in the East and have come to worship Him...And when they had come into the house, they saw the young child with Mary His mother, and fell down and worshiped Him. And when they had opened their

treasures, they presented gifts to Him: gold, frankincense, and myrrh" (Matthew 2:1-2, 11 NKJV).

They set out on a journey to worship the newborn child and to honor Him with expensive gifts. Their act of reverence and generosity came from their hearts. For years they had anticipated the arrival of the Savior of the world. Herod attempted to highjack the mission of the wise men by demanding that they kidnap the homeless baby and bring him back to the King. Herod's pride didn't allow him to seek out and submit to someone greater; rather, he saw Jesus as a threat and sought to destroy Him. "Now when they had departed, behold, an angel of the Lord appeared to Joseph in a dream, saying, 'Arise, take the young child and His mother, flee to Egypt, and stay there until I bring you word; for Herod will seek the young child to destroy Him'" (Matthew 2:13 NKJV).

Just as we anticipate and enjoy Almighty God's gifts, others who are intimated by bowing to a Savior will seek ways to put a damper on or even destroy our faith expressions. But in a spirit of humility and love, we still worship Jesus with a grateful heart for His extravagant gift of salvation. He came to seek and to save all who receive His grace. We need His grace to live lives full of forgiveness and love. When people try to kill your joy, remember the joy that Jesus brings to the world and count on the joy yet to come.

Anticipate God's generous gifts, but be wise about future expectations. We must not spend money we do not have just because our economic future is bright. Perhaps we increase our standard of giving and not our standard of living. Anticipation for what God wants is the best way to follow His will. Most of all, we anticipate growing in oneness with the One who loves us the most—Jesus Christ.

Heavenly Father, I anticipate Your great love for great things from You yet to come, in Christ's name, amen.

TAKEAWAY: *Relational leaders anticipate God's generous gifts but are wise about future expectations.*

Summary of Chapter Twenty-Two Takeaways

1. Relational leaders are hopeful for a better future.

2. Relational leaders anticipate where God is at work and join Him.

3. Relational leaders anticipate God's generous gifts but are wise about future expectations.

Chapter Twenty-Three

Create a Safe Home Environment

*By wisdom a house is built, and through understanding
it is established; through knowledge its rooms are
filled with rare and beautiful treasures.*

PROVERBS 24:3-4

*Home is where everyone comes for respite and rest, but
if a home environment does not provide the love that
children need, then they will seek it elsewhere.*

NICOLINE AMBE

Jesus Affirmed Hugs of Healing

Do not be afraid to hug at home. Hugs bring healing. Sons and daughters need the secure embrace of their dad and the comforting caress of their mom. Jesus tells of one particularly famous hug—the father's hug of the prodigal son: "While he was still a long way off, his father saw him and was filled with compassion for him; he ran to his son, threw his arms around him and kissed him" (Luke 15:20). A child may be conflicted by a feeling of inadequacy or a fear of public embarrassment. It's in this state of uncertainty that a kind hug communicates care and concern. Shed your stoic aloofness and convey your affection.

There is no need to conceal one's need for affection, as these desires come from our divine design. God made us with a tender heart that needs the heartfelt connection from another. Affectionate desires require a touch on the arm, holding hands, a kiss on the check, a pat on the back, or a loving hug. Arms are meant to extend often—like the Lord does toward His needy children. "My hand will sustain him; surely my arm will strengthen him" (Psalms 89:21).

A heart full of compassion can't help but hug. When you feel the need to physically communicate acceptance and love, you hug. However, hugs should not be a hugger's way to get his or her needs met; rather, it is an unselfish act to meet another's need for comfort and love. Hugs are not meant to smother, but to breathe life into a loved one. Thus, hug often for someone else's sake.

> **Point to Ponder:** A heart full of compassion can't help but hug.

Hugs can communicate forgiveness because they are an invitation into intimacy. You invite someone to enter into your present world and forget the misunderstandings of the past. Your silent hug of a hurting heart becomes heaven's vessel for healing. We flush out cold aloneness and fear with a warm embrace. Tears of relief flow from the eyes of a person cradled in the arms of compassion. "Then he [Joseph] threw his arms around his brother Benjamin and wept, and Benjamin embraced him, weeping. And he kissed all his brothers and wept over them" (Genesis 45:14-15a).

People cannot hug themselves. Use your unselfish hugs as an advertisement for Jesus. Explain how the compassion of Christ compels you to embrace with eternal energy. Be generous with your emotions and experience hugging's healing dividends. "As a father has compassion on his children, so the Lord has compassion on those who fear him" (Psalm 103:13). Ask yourself: Who in my life needs a regular embrace of comfort and compassion? From whom do I need regular hugs?

> **TAKEAWAY:** Relational leaders who are generous with their emotions experience healing.

Fishing for a Relational Experience

Our grandson Harrison just celebrated his sixth birthday. Among his bounty of presents, his favorite was a red-and-black Zebco rod and reel, accompanied by a tiny tackle box. "Pop, I want you to take me fishing." Who can say no to that sweet solicitation? So, three days later, Harrison and I woke up early and I gave him a lesson on rigging his line by tying a fishing knot. In spite of the 38 degree Farenheit morning, we made our way to the pond near our house and "wet a hook" for about 90 minutes. There were no big bass to be found (though Harrison was sure two hit his bait but got away), but it was no matter, because our shared memory of love, adventure, and yes, patience, will be stuffed and mounted in our minds and on our hearts forever.

Point to Ponder: *Relational family experiences lodge deep in our memories.*

Jesus's would-be disciples were a motley crew of fishermen. Then He said to them, "Follow Me, and I will make you fishers of men" (Matthew 4:19 NKJV). Rugged, rough, and weather-beaten, these men took their life lessons of hard work and faith and followed Jesus. Just as the Lord had given them the resources and skills to fish in the natural world of physical provision, now Christ would equip and empower them to fish for souls in the supernatural world of spiritual provision. Jesus was clear: if they would take a step of faith to follow Him—He would make them fishers of men. Competency comes with Christ's calling.

The good news of Jesus's love and forgiveness is tasty bait for those who believe. Your imperfect life of love and forgiveness gives you the credibility to cast the net of Christ's love over lives in need of a Savior. When you first believed, you began your journey with Jesus for the purpose of helping wayward souls find rest in a relationship with Christ. Following Jesus requires fishing with Jesus. Show up for others, be generous, cast the gospel net, and God will fill it with souls. Fishing with Jesus takes time and requires patience, but you come to know Him much better in the process.

The beauty of fishing with Jesus is the opportunity to grow in your intimacy with the One who loves you the most. You learn from His example of how to love people well, and you grow in your confidence to share His gospel of love and forgiveness. Soon enough, with Paul, you'll be able to say, "For I am not ashamed of the Gospel (good news) of Christ, for it is God's power working unto salvation [for deliverance from eternal death] to everyone who believes with a personal trust and a confident surrender and firm reliance, to the Jew first and also to the Greek" (Romans 1:16 AMPC). When you fish with Jesus, you are on the front lines of sharing faith. That simple act grows your faith and understanding in God's love and wisdom. A day of fishing with Jesus may not result in a soul caught for Christ, but joy and fulfillment will be stuffed and mounted in your heart and mind forever.

Heavenly Father, as I follow Jesus, grow my boldness
to share the gospel. In Jesus's name, amen.

TAKEAWAY: *Relational leaders create mutually enjoyable experiences in order to grow relationships.*

Home Sweet Home

What type of home does the Lord bless? He blesses a home that trusts Him and does right as God defines it. God blesses a home that implements heaven's agenda on earth. God blesses a home that builds up rather than tears down. God blesses a home that humbly reads Scripture together and seeks to personally apply its truth. "The Lord's curse is on the house of the wicked, but he blesses the home of the righteous" (Proverbs 3:33).

Point to Ponder: God blesses a home that prays, plays, worships, and serves together.

God blesses a home that prays together, plays together, worships together, and serves together. "God bless our home" is a wise prayer for a family of faith. Even if your home is more like hell than heaven, you can still make a significant difference. Let your light of love shine in service to undeserving family members and your heavenly Father will draw them unto Himself.

Perhaps you are the spiritual leader of the home, but you do not have the confidence to lead in religious matters. Yet, there is hope. First of all, keep it simple by spending individual time alone with the Lord. Take what He is teaching you in His Word and transfer it to your family. If you are learning humility, read a Bible verse about the humble, and share a recent humbling experience from your life. Declare these words with Joshua from the Bible: "If serving the LORD seems undesirable to you, then choose for yourselves this day whom you will serve, whether the gods your ancestors served beyond the Euphrates, or the gods of the Amorites, in whose land you are living. But as for me and my household, we will serve the LORD" (Joshua 24:15).

God blesses the leader of the home who is authentic and accountable. Family members can relate to your real struggles, while they probably cannot relate to you if they think you have no struggles at all. The home is heaven's hospital for healing, encouragement, and accountability. Make Christianity work at home, and then you have the credibility of a God-blessed model to export into the church and community. "By wisdom a house is built, and through understanding it is established" (Proverbs 24:3). Ask yourself: how, by God's grace, can I make our home a haven of rest and righteous behavior?

TAKEAWAY: *God blesses relational leaders who are authentic and accountable at home.*

Relational Parents Help Their Children Feel Safe at Home

There are many simple ways you can help make a child feel whole and happy in the home. Here are a few to consider:

Don't Yell

Take a moment and think back to the last time someone yelled at you. How did it make you feel? It probably made you feel sad or angry or maybe even both. No one likes to be yelled at, and children are certainly no exception. We all get things wrong sometimes or make a less than perfect decision. Children should be taught that it's okay to make a mistake without worrying about feeling shamed or attacked. Shouting can cause fear and reciprocal anger in children and may adversely affect general communication with them.

Let Kids Be Kids

Playtime is absolutely necessary for learning good motor and social skills. That's not to say they should be free to hang off the ceiling fan or draw on the walls, but children need the freedom to explore their surroundings and express themselves in an appropriate physical way. It is crucial to proper development. Encourage their curiosity and creativity by allowing them to discover their world in a safe, controlled manner.

Read to Them

Reading aloud to young children is often cited as the single most important thing you can do to ensure they develop the language skills they'll need to be an effective communicator later in life. You can start even before they can talk. Exposing them to books at a young age will better prepare them for school and grow their imaginations.

Set a Good Example

Children notice everything. They hear and see things we sometimes think they don't. Always be aware of your actions and words in the presence of children. We may not think they are concerned with everything we say and do, but in reality, they absorb much more than we sometimes imagine.

Stay Positive

We all face challenges in life, and often we respond to those challenges in a negative way. When unexpected difficulties arise, it can be easy to forget that having a negative attitude will likely only lead to further negativity in the future. Don't let it become a pattern. If your children see you respond to something negatively they will be more inclined to react negatively as well.

Be Consistent

For patterns of good behavior to develop, be consistent in your approach to childcare. These strategies will do no good if a child is confused about what is expected of them. It's important to know how they behave in external environments, too, so take some time to get to know their teachers, day care staff, or after school program leader—wherever they spend the most time out of the home.

Be Honest and Straightforward

Phrases like "because I said so" or "those are just the rules" are unhelpful to a child trying to navigate the confusing intricacies of how to be a part of society. Explain to them why these things are important. Although it may feel easiest to rush through awkward conversations with your child, resist the urge to do so. Build your bond by leveling with them. They will respect you for it and relate better to others as a result.

Display Affection

The importance of displaying affection can't be overestimated. Hug. Cuddle. Show concern when they are upset and ask questions about why they are feeling that way. Talk to them about their day or things they like. Allow them to express their feelings and let them see yours. Showing your child that you love and care for them helps foster their ability to develop empathy for others.[4]

Summary of Chapter Twenty-Three Takeaways

1. Relational leaders who are generous with their emotions experience healing.

2. Relational leaders create mutually enjoyable experiences in order to grow relationships.

3. God blesses relational leaders who are authentic and accountable at home.

Chapter Twenty-Four

Serve Without Expecting to Be Served

The Son of Man did not come to be served,
but to serve.

MATTHEW 20:28

God determines your greatness by how many people
you serve, not how many people serve you.

RICK WARREN

Jesus Modeled Selfless Service

He served the least and the greatest; He served the sinners and the saints; He served the rich and the poor; He served singles and He served families; He served mad people and He served glad people; He served when He was tired and He served when He was rested. You could not out-serve Jesus because His service was motivated and fueled by His heavenly Father. Intimacy with the Almighty compels us to serve. Relational leaders cultivate a habit of serving others.

Ironically, Jesus served others even at the point of His greatest need. When engulfed in His own personal crisis, He chose to serve others instead of being served. The night before facing imminent death, He served by washing feet. Use this same selfless strategy of service, and watch the world run to Jesus. In the middle of your own Last Supper experience, serve. When you are rejected, serve instead of retaliating. When you are forgotten, serve instead of feeling sorry for yourself. When you are hurt, serve instead of allowing your heart to harden.

Serve for Jesus's sake and not your own. Make it a lifetime goal to out-serve all with whom you come into contact, especially those closest to you. An attitude of service is others-centered and Christ-focused. You can't out-serve Christ, but you can be a conduit of service on His behalf. Seek to out-serve others for your Savior. Serving others is essential for relational leaders because it makes others feel important and valued.

> **TAKEAWAY:** Relational leaders who serve without expecting to be served grow a culture of selflessness at home and at work.

Relational Leaders Selflessly Serve

Joy comes when we join Jesus in giving away our life without expecting anything in return.

Parents do this every day—they serve those who can't (and sometimes won't) serve them. Parents wipe bottoms, wipe runny noses, wipe food-crusted faces (though not necessarily in that order), all out of love and devotion to their little gifts from God. Barbara Bush rocked the cradle of a president of the United States—perhaps she prayed something like the following for her son George W. prior to his days in the White House, when as a young man he battled with alcohol abuse:

> *Dear Lord, bring my boy back to You. I have done everything humanly possible to selflessly love and serve him. He is Your child, Your creation, so I trust You to do whatever it takes to awaken him out of his sinful slumber and draw Him by Your Spirit to see himself as You see him: forgiven, loved, and precious in Your sight. Thank You, Father. In Jesus's name, amen.*

Her prayers were answered, and her son was able to complete his God-given assignment to become the leader of the free world. Sometimes our best service is to pray for someone and trust the Lord to do a work of grace in their hearts. Prayer serves the Lord's greater purposes in His timing and for His glory. We serve with success when we selflessly pray for other hearts to know God's heart.

Point to Ponder: *Selfless service is found in earnest prayer for a lost soul.*

What Does It Mean to Lead by Serving Without Expecting Anything in Return?

The job description of successful leaders is service to others. It is not jockeying for position, nor is it maneuvering for power. Instead, it is positioning oneself to serve. This will obviously be challenging for the insecure soul in need of abundant attention! Servant leaders avoid the limelight and serve in ways that many times go unnoticed. It is the little things that make a servant leader. It may be taking out the trash at home or making the coffee at work.

No task is too menial for the servant leader, but there is something bigger than behavior that distinguishes a servant leader: attitude. A servant leader always asks how she can make others successful. He or she knows that if those around them are successful then there is a good chance they will experience success. They are wise to want what's best for others.

Self-service, on the other hand, builds a culture of mediocrity. If it is all about taking care of my little world, then I am not giving any thought to the needs of other team members. That creates a culture of every man for himself or survival of the fittest. This self-service contributes to a scarcity mentality. One starts to fear—if I serve you then you might look better than me and you might get all the credit. This fear of not being noticed facilitates competition instead of cooperation.

TAKEAWAY: *Relational leaders avoid attention and serve in ways that many times go unnoticed.*

Selfless Leaders Share the Credit for Success

Selfless leadership is not caught up with getting the credit. The servant leader has put to death the need for self-recognition. The servant leader is happy for attention and credit to go to others. This is the place where attention and credit belong, because our humility cannot handle the attention. Servant leadership resists this temptation to linger in the limelight. Instead, the servant leader may give away opportunities that come his or her way. Seek to serve others and let status find you when the Lord deems you ready.

Jesus served quietly on most occasions and boldly as needed. No sincere seeker was neglected. His motive was to serve for the glory of God. His ultimate service was laying down His life for the human race. Consequently, followers of Christ can become better servant leaders because Jesus seeks to serve through them. You can't accomplish this alone, but He can serve through you.

Submit to Him and watch Him use you to serve. Let go of getting attention and credit and instead celebrate the success of others. Quietly volunteer for the next lowly task. Set up others to succeed. Give away your life and you will find it. This is the way of Christ. This is the way to serve and lead. Submit to God, serve people—and others will follow! As Jesus says, "If your first concern is to look after yourself, you'll never find yourself. But if you forget about yourself and look to me, you'll find both yourself and me" (Matthew 10:39 MSG).

TAKEAWAY: *Relational leaders look for ways to honor and give credit to Jesus and others.*

Selfless Leaders Serve at Home

"Now that I, your Lord and Teacher, have washed your feet, you also should wash one another's feet. I have set you an example that you should do as I have done for you" (John 13:14-15).

My mother-in-law is a stroke victim. But for 55 years, Jean outserved James, my father-in-law. Many, many times he has expressed to me and our children how his sweetie selflessly served him with a tone and tenor that brought great joy to her and a grateful heart to him. She paid bills on time, she was present for school activities for Timmy and Rita, their son and daughter. She provided a clean, and more importantly, caring, home. Jean lavished her family with her loving smile and stunningly attractive servant spirit. She made appetizing and plentiful meals so that we could enjoy them in a relaxing, supportive environment. But then the stroke happened.

Strokes restrict life-giving blood. In Jean's case, her brain suffered from a temporary cessation of blood flow. It only took a short-term shortage of blood to the brain to cause long-term limitations to her speech and physical mobility. Speech therapy helped some, but today, after five years, though her mind is clear, she is unable to express her thoughts verbally. Now Jean requires James to serve her in the selfless ways she served him for so many years.

My father-in-law loves his bride with a heart of gratitude and with his hands in selfless service. "She has served me all these years, I am honored to serve her. My purpose in life is to be there for her when she is afraid, frustrated, and unable to take care of herself." James now outserves Jean because he cherishes her and wants to honor her. His service compels me to love well!

> **Point to Ponder:** Marriages grow richer when husband and wife look to out-serve the other.

Selfless Service Flushes Out Selfish Demands

Out-serve your spouse. This does not come naturally to our selfish selves, but if you do this you will start to see positive differences in both of you. Service makes your spouse feel loved and respected and makes you feel fulfilled and significant. Unappreciated service can wear you down over time, but trust God. Allow Him to supply the strength for your service. If the Lord is not empowering your service, you will eventually burn out and possibly become resentful. Bitter service does not last, but joyful service does.

Serve your spouse out of gratitude to God for giving them to you. Serve them in the everyday routines of life and when they least expect it. Serve them where they want to be served, not just where you want to serve them. Service might be unloading the dishwasher, taking out the garbage, mowing the lawn, maintaining the house, or taking care of the cars. Their service may include an organized family, dinner at home, being on time, keeping a calendar, or planning a trip. If you are unsure, ask them how they like to be served. Relational husbands and wives serve one another how the other wants to be served.

Selfless Leaders Serve at Work

Carry this attitude of out-serving into your occupation. Be one who serves in the workplace, especially if you are a leader or manager. Quietly and clandestinely clean up the break room and even wipe out the gooey microwave. Service from a sincere heart values and respects others. Our Savior modeled service. He did not come to be served, but to serve and to give His very own life as the ultimate act of service. When we enlist in the service of God's kingdom, we become His full-time servants. Service for our Savior is a thread that runs through the life of everyone who is led by the Lord. If Jesus is your model for leadership and living life, you see how essential it is for relational leaders to serve without expecting to be served.

> **Point to Ponder:** *Service from a sincere heart values and respects others.*

Summary of Chapter Twenty-Four Takeaways

1. Relational leaders who serve without expecting to be served grow a selfless culture at home and work.

2. Relational leaders avoid attention and serve in ways that many times go unnoticed.

3. Relational leaders look for ways to honor and give credit to Jesus and others.

Chapter Twenty-Five

Serve with a
Second-Mile Mindset

*You, my brothers and sisters, were called to be
free. But do not use your freedom to indulge the
flesh; rather, serve one another humbly in love.*

Galatians 5:13

*No one is useless in this world who
lightens the burdens of another.*

Charles Dickens

Jesus Taught That We Should Do More Than Is Expected

If anyone forces you to go one mile, go with them two miles" (Matthew 5:41). It's much easier to help someone I like than someone I don't like. If I enjoy a person's company, it is a joy to listen to their dreams or offer them advice about a difficult decision they face. I confess that some days I only want to serve someone who one day might remember my good deed and offer to serve me in return. However, I am called to do more than is expected without expecting anything in return. I am called to second-mile service.

> **Point to Ponder:** A loving servant leader does more for the unlovable than is expected.

Jesus illustrates this concept of second-mile service. He instructs His disciples to carry the load of another twice as far as expected, even if you loathe them. In this instance, it was the despised Roman soldier who had the legal right to indiscriminately demand a citizen carry

193

their weighted backpack for a mile. Even if the unsuspecting individual was traveling in the opposite direction, they could be enlisted on the spot to assist the soldier. The second-mile service Jesus describes requires selfless sacrifice. Paul took on this challenge as well: "Though I am free and belong to no one, I have made myself a slave to everyone, to win as many as possible" (1 Corinthians 9:19). Love does more than is expected for the unlovable.

If your boss has a demanding demeanor or unrealistic expectations, do your work as "unto the Lord" (Colossians 3:23), praying for God's grace to do your very best. Learn to look outside your immediate resources to other friends or colleagues who might lend their expertise. Do more than is expected by engaging a mentor who is experienced in the new role you have been assigned. Your second-mile job attitude honors your Savior Jesus.

Generosity with our time and money is another way we can do more than expected. Giving is an expression of our gratitude to God for His incredible blessings. Perhaps we give more than our allocated time to a seeking stranger who needs direction for their life and work. Or, a young person may need our encouragement to get established. When we are generous with our calendar and cash, we go the second mile in our relational investments. Thus, we give more than is expected to those God puts in our path.

Heavenly Father, grow my heart of generosity
into one that exceeds expectations.

TAKEAWAY: *Relational leaders who are generous with their calendar and cash go the second mile in their relational investments.*

Relational Leaders Have a Second-Mile Business Mindset

Chick-fil-A is a company consisting of many relational leaders. In an article from the *Christian Post*, which describes the company's second-mile mindset in their culture of service, we read this:

> It isn't entirely a new concept. In fact, he didn't even come up with it. Jesus did. But it's clear that Dan Cathy, President and Chief Operating Officer for Chick-fil-A, lives by the idea behind second mile service. Matthew 5:41 says, "If someone forces you to go one mile, go with him two..."
>
> In addition to second mile service, the secrets to their success include listening to the customer, focusing on getting better before trying to get bigger, and placing an emphasis on quality. The philosophy and mission of the company is to "glorify God by being a faithful steward to all that is entrusted to us. To have a positive influence on all who come in contact with Chick-fil-A."[5]

Relational Leaders Exceed Expectations

"Confident of your obedience, I write to you, knowing that you will do even more than I ask" (Philemon 1:21). God has exceeded expectations in His interactions with us. He has done what He said and more. There is nothing halfway about God. He does things right and then throws in a little bit extra just to overwhelm us with His grace. When God or others ask something of you, go for it with gusto. Exceed expectations. Exceed expectations because God has done the same for you. Make it a goal to bring more than you get to a relationship.

If someone asks for prayer, pray right then and there. Make it a habit to pray regularly for those in need, especially those who request prayer. Exceed expectations in your prayer for others. Exceed expectations in your work. Work not just to get by with the minimum required effort, but in order to give glory to God. What better way to make Christianity attractive than to work with excellence? When you exceed expectations, you open the door for others to inquire about your motivation—the Lord Jesus.

Point to Ponder: *Make it a goal to bring more value to a relationship than you receive.*

Exceeding expectations may help advance your career. People want to work with and for someone who goes the second mile. They want to reward and hang out with someone who exceeds expectations. When we exceed expectations, we know that, at the very least, the One we serve will be satisfied. Lastly, exceed expectations with your attitude. A positive and "can do" attitude goes a long way. There are a lot of things we cannot control, but our attitude is one we can. Go over the top with an attitude of gratitude and generosity. Just like Paul says about the Macedonians, "For I testify that they gave as much as they were able, and even beyond their ability" (2 Corinthians 8:3). Be exceedingly grateful!

Marriage is another arena in which you can serve beyond what is expected. It is the first relational opportunity to offer love and respect. No one in marriage has ever complained of too much love and respect. It is not possible to overly respect or overly love your spouse. Look for creative ways to love and respect them beyond their expectations. Exceeding expectations in the home makes for harmony and contentment. The home is all about others, not you.

There are times you feel the need to be spoiled, but first seek to spoil and serve others. You receive blessings and encouragement beyond measure when you serve in ways that exceed others' expectations. It is not a game of keeping score of who has done the most for the other lately. Rather, marriage is about dying to your own expectations so that you can exceed the expectations of your spouse and children. You have the option to exceed what God expects of you. Model this second-mile mentality for them. Go more than one mile for another by giving others what they don't "deserve." Exceed expectations for heaven's sake.

Surrender to God Your Entire Life

Why just get by with God? A prayer of salvation is the beginning of belief and a lifetime love affair with the Lord. He has a treasure trove of adventure waiting for those who will take Him at His Word and dare to exceed His expectations. So, if God asks for 10% giving, you want to exceed His minimum requirement. If He asks for one day of Sabbath, you want to give Him daily mini-Sabbaths. If He asks for your heart, you want to give Him your life. Those who surrender their entire life to the Lord will grow into relational leaders. Again, the Macedonians provide us an example. Paul writes, "And they exceeded our expectations: They gave themselves first of all to the Lord, and then by the will of God also to us" (2 Corinthians 8:5).

> *Heavenly Father, by Your grace I want to*
> *exceed expectations in my service for You.*

TAKEAWAY: *Relational leaders go more than one mile for others by giving them more than they deserve.*

Relational Leaders Acknowledge God's Appointment

An anointed leader is chosen by God, not self-appointed or randomly assigned to a position by man. The example of David comes to mind. "So [Jesse] sent for [David] and had him brought in. He was glowing with health and had a fine appearance and handsome features. Then the Lord said, 'Rise and anoint him; this is the one.' So Samuel took the horn of oil and anointed him in the presence of his brothers, and from that day on the Spirit of the Lord came powerfully upon David" (1 Samuel 16:12-13). An anointed leader knows they are called by God, not driven by selfish ambition or the desire to be great. Greatness is reserved for servants of the Lord who quietly give themselves to purposes greater than themselves. If I strive to be seen or selected for a role, I miss a chance to grow my faith while waiting on the will of God to unfold. Leaders who feel entitled feel the need for a job title so they seem important, while anointed leaders esteem others as more important.

Point to Ponder: Greatness is reserved for servants of the Lord who quietly give themselves to purposes greater than themselves.

David was minding his own business—being faithful in his call to shepherd well—when the Lord called him to shepherd His flock. God's choice was probably a surprise to those who expected a "better" résumé for a king, but God in His wisdom selected a servant with a love for God and a fiery heart to defend and lead God's people. Samuel, the man of God, followed the Lord's leading by anointing David in front of his brothers. Because of their faith, submission, and obedience—the Spirit of the Lord came powerfully upon God's anointed. "I have found David my servant; with my sacred oil I have anointed him. My hand will sustain him; surely my arm will strengthen him" (Psalm 89:20-21).

Are you waiting for an opportunity you think is just right for you? Or are you looking and praying for just the right person to serve with you? In either situation, be patient, prayerful, and openhanded. Trust Jesus and wait on His best. It is better to be in a storm with Jesus asleep in the boat than to be on the shore without Him. At any moment, Christ can calm the chaos and bring clarity to the confusion—so avoid getting ahead of God. You bring the most glory to the Lord when your joy and contentment are found in Christ and not your circumstances.

The power to lead is not primarily about position but submission. Submission positions you to receive favor from your Savior Jesus. Submit to God's Spirit to cleanse your heart, fill your soul, and lead your life. Submit to the authorities in your life to validate your ideas, protect you from yourself, and hold you responsible to steward well the mission of your organization. Anointed leadership leads out of weakness while leaning into the Spirit for strength. Is your faith fatigued? Ask the Lord for a fresh anointing. Be prepared and trust God that in Christ you are anointed as His relational leader. As Paul says, "Now it is God who makes both us and you stand firm in Christ. He anointed us, set his seal of ownership on us, and put His Spirit in our hearts as a deposit, guaranteeing what is to come" (2 Corinthians 1:21-22).

Heavenly Father, I submit to You, bend my will to Your
will and by Your Spirit anoint me for Your service.

TAKEAWAY: *Relational leaders focus on submission to Christ, not their own power.*

Summary of Chapter Twenty-Five Takeaways

1. Relational leaders who are generous with their calendar and cash go the second mile in their relational investments.

2. Relational leaders go more than one mile for others by giving them more than they deserve.

3. Relational leaders focus on submission to Christ, not their own power.

Chapter Twenty-Six

Serve Your Way Out of Discouragement

It was just before the Passover Festival. Jesus knew that the hour had come for him to leave this world and go to the Father. Having loved his own who were in the world, he loved them to the end...He poured water into a basin and began to wash his disciples' feet, drying them with the towel that was wrapped around him.

JOHN 13:1, 5

Our role as leaders is to turn away from our disappointment and abandonment and give ourselves to those with whom we still have influence.

COSTA MITCHELL

Jesus Served in the Face of Discouragement

Discouragement invites relational leaders to lead. It is your time to trust the Lord and lead by faith, not fear. In hard times, a leader asks, "Will I panic or pray?" "Will I stay calm or be sucked into the chaos?" "Will I serve the team or stay secluded in silence?" Jesus faced death, but He was determined to stay focused on His heavenly Father and the mission at hand and served even in the face of certain death: "After that, he poured water into a basin and began to wash his disciples' feet, drying them with the towel that was wrapped around him" (John 13:5). Adversity is an opportunity to prove that Christ is in control.

> **Point to Ponder:** Discouragement invites relational leaders to lead.

How can you use adversity to your advantage as a leader? One way is to unify the team around common objectives and goals. There is no better way to bring people together than in times of hardship and difficulty. In fact, you probably will not succeed without the team rising to the next level of leadership and team support. Reward creativity, because innovation can lead your team past limitations. Lead the team to accomplish more with less.

Use difficult times to create a culture of hard work and honesty. Paul said, "We put no stumbling block in anyone's path, so that our ministry will not be discredited. Rather, as servants of God we commend ourselves in every way: in great endurance; in troubles, hardships and distresses" (2 Corinthians 6:3-4). Difficult times may mean longer hours and less pay. Invite honest feedback so you can improve your process and products. Raise team expectations from "surviving" to "thriving."

Serve at home and work with appreciation. It is easy to demand more and more while under pressure and forget to say, "Thank you." Perhaps give the team a day off, leave a grateful voicemail, buy everyone lunch, or send flowers. Relational leaders honestly inquire, "How can I out-serve others, especially in the face of misfortune?" "Where do I need to take responsibility, instead of blaming outside forces?" Relational leaders model the way of service when the team is feeling discouraged. As Jesus said, "I have set you an example that you should do as I have done for you" (John 13:15).

TAKEAWAY: *Relational leaders raise team expectations from surviving to thriving.*

When in Doubt

I remember feeling doubt when I was diagnosed with early stage prostate cancer. I was mad because I felt betrayed by God—how could He allow this disease to cause me so much distress? After all, my life was committed to serving the Lord, and now with raw abruptness, was my time on earth all of a sudden expired? I was sad because I wanted to walk my youngest daughter down the aisle, but I feared that cancer would deny me that joyous opportunity. Doubt almost destroyed my faith, until my patient heavenly Father reminded me of His plan. God desired to do a work of grace in me so that He could love others through me.

Doubt seeks to destroy our faith. In our discouragement or even despair we begin to question God. "What did I do wrong?" "Lord, did You call me to this place of confusion?" "Where is my joy and hope?" "Are You even real or just a figment of my imagination?" Without intervention, doubt crushes our faith in Christ. Relational leaders use doubt for relational depth with God and others. They confess their doubt and lean into the Lord's assurance and the support of their community.

> **Point to Ponder:** God desires to do a work of grace in you so that He can love others through you.

Fortunately, faith does not have to take a furlough when we are frustrated and fatigued. It is in our confinement that Christ wants to remind us of His great power. Cry out to Him in your confused circumstances and He will earnestly listen in love. "In my distress I called to the LORD; I called out to my God. From his temple he heard my voice; my cry came to his ears" (2 Samuel 22:7). He does not leave His loved ones alone and in doubt.

It Is Okay to Be in Doubt

It is okay to be in doubt, but it is not okay to remain in doubt. What doubt challenges your faith in God? Is it His provision, His promises, His presence, His character, or His care? When these questions assault your confidence in Christ, take a step back and review His track record. The reality of His work in your life can restore you to a productive mindset of peace and forgiveness. Years of answered prayer are proof enough of His love and concern.

Furthermore, use this temporary time of distrust to go deeper with Jesus. The pressure you feel on all sides is your Savior's way of soliciting your attention. When in doubt, seek out the Lord, learn to love Him completely, and discern more fully His profound promises. Use doubt to dig deeper into the truth of Scripture; marinate your mind in God's Word. "Taste and see that the LORD is good; blessed is the man who takes refuge in him" (Psalm 34:8).

When in doubt, stay steadfast in seeking your Savior. Wait on Him, especially when you wonder what is next. Where there is true faith, you might also have times of unbelief; so remain faithful, even when questions arise. Perseverance will one day free you to be a stronger and more committed follower of Christ. See Jesus for who He is. Doubt dissolves in His reassuring presence. Doubt starves to death when it is not fed. Relational leaders do not deny doubt, but persevere in hope, faith, and love. "Blessed are those whose help is the God of Jacob, whose hope is in the LORD his God. He is the Maker of heaven and earth, the sea, and everything in them—he remains faithful forever" (Psalm 146:5-6).

Heavenly Father, help me in my unbelief to believe You are all I need during this time of intense uncertainty. In Jesus's name, amen.

TAKEAWAY: *Relational leaders recognize that it is okay to doubt but not to remain in doubt.*

Courage Conquers Discouragement

"Have I not commanded you? Be strong and courageous. Do not be afraid; do not be discouraged, for the LORD your God will be with you wherever you go" (Joshua 1:9). With these words, Moses encouraged Joshua. It takes courage to wake up, get up, and face the day. Issues and people may make us feel afraid, but with God's grace we face our fears by faith. Fear is not absent from a courageous spirit—it's just not in control. Fear may be a loud passenger in the back seat shouting concerns, but it is not driving the car; courage holds the steering wheel. We must minimize our fears of the unknown and maximize our faith in the known. Cowards are intimidated by fear and become passive, while faith inspires the courageous to carry on.

> **Point to Ponder:** *Cowards are intimidated by fear and become passive, while faith inspires the courageous to carry on.*

What barriers do you face that courage can help you overcome? Maybe you feel undervalued at work and it is time to ask for a raise. Perhaps you need to tell a friend "no" and risk hurting their feelings or even jeopardizing your friendship. It may be your responsibility to lovingly confront a strong leader about their inappropriate conduct. You might need courage to continue your education, remain committed to your marriage, or stand up to a bully. These are all noble pursuits. Bravery teaches us to stay engaged. Ezra was encouraged with these words, applicable also to us: "Rise up; this matter is in your hands. We will support you, so take courage and do it" (Ezra 10:4).

Leaders can courageously find answers or make excuses in cowardice. This is why a decisive leader with average skills is superior to an indecisive leader with greater skills. Courage causes the one in charge to move forward even when not all the facts are known. Courageous leaders know how to adjust as more data is discovered, but all the while they lead the team toward the goal. A leader with grit and guts doesn't panic, but perseveres. They follow where Almighty God leads. Relational leaders ask Christ for courage and, in turn, use that courage at work and home.

We are wise to gain our courage from Christ. He who modeled courage in the face of the most horrific circumstances gives us what we need to face our fears. His wisdom gives us insight to overcome ignorance. His grace gives us patience to outlast another's procrastination or prevarication. His love gives us undaunted leadership to lead with compassion and clarity. Thus, we find courage to pray. We feel the support of God's people and their prayers. Our courage, though imperfect, keeps us focused on our perfect Savior Jesus. Courage exalts Him! As Paul said, "I eagerly expect and hope that I will in no way be ashamed, but will have sufficient courage so that now as always Christ will be exalted in my body, whether by life or by death" (Philippians 1:20).

Heavenly Father, give me courage to do the
next right thing and to totally trust You.

TAKEAWAY: *A decisive relational leader with average skills is superior to an indecisive leader with greater skills.*

Summary of Chapter Twenty-Six Takeaways

1. Relational leaders raise team expectations from surviving to thriving.

2. Relational leaders recognize that it is okay to doubt but not to remain in doubt.

3. A decisive relational leader with average skills is superior to an indecisive leader with greater skills.

Chapter Twenty-Seven

Listen with a Desire to Understand and Help

Speak, Lord, for your servant is listening.

1 Samuel 3:9

Everyday, we have to ask God for our assignment, we must not assume we understand His plan but rather surrender to His will daily...God speaks in a soft voice I can hear better when I resolve to listen and stop putting words in His mouth. Prayer is communication.

E'yen A. Gardner

Jesus Spent Time in Prayer Listening to His Father

You know the story. Jesus and the disciples had just fed 5,000 men and at least another 5,000 women and children.

> Immediately Jesus made the disciples get into the boat and go on ahead of him to the other side, while he dismissed the crowd. After he had dismissed them, he went up on a mountainside by himself to pray. Later that night, he was there alone, and the boat was already a considerable distance from land, buffeted by the waves because the wind was against it. Shortly before dawn Jesus went out to them, walking on the lake. (Matthew 14:22-25)

What a miracle, what an extraordinary time to call attention to what just happened! Instead, the disciples—with jaws gaping in amazement—were dismissed by Jesus to their next faith adventure on a nautical field trip to the other side of the lake. While scratching their head in wonderment, Jesus proceeded to dismiss the crowd with full stomachs, as He made His way up the mountain to pray. The Son of God needed time with His Father for refreshment.

If I had just experienced this kind of miracle, I would have probably called a press conference and let the whole world know through social media. I need to be reminded that my experience of success is not the time to feed my pride and ego, but to steady my soul in prayer. Exhausted from success, Jesus refreshed himself in prayer and prepared His heart to be ready for His next assignment. Having prayed and received the love of His Father, Jesus made His way down the mountain to the edge of the lake. He then walked on water toward the disciples, who were gripped by fear. Like Jesus, do you pause to pray? Has your heart been prepared by prayer for your next season of service so you might "walk on water" to calm people who are fearful and feeling alone?

> **Point to Ponder:** We are most vulnerable to temptation when we experience success. In the time of temptation, we are in desperate need of being still and listening to our heavenly Father.

Relational Leaders Intently Listen to the Lord

"Let the person who is able to hear, listen to *and follow* what the Spirit proclaims to all the churches" (Revelation 3:22 THE VOICE). I am learning to talk less and listen more in my time with the Lord. My goal is to go to my heavenly Father daily and actively listen to His heart— what Christ says is the most vital communication I have all day. Wisdom says to start the day listening for divine direction so as to avoid pride's pitfalls and unproductive paths. When I first listen to heaven's heart, I am more effective engaging hearts on earth. When I actively listen to the Almighty, His Spirit flushes out my selfish pride and replaces it with selfless humility. I can listen best when I have been listening to Jesus. The One who created our ears gives us ears to hear.

> **Point to Ponder:** When I first listen to heaven's heart, I am more effective engaging hearts on earth.

A Life-Changing Prayer Walk

A few years back I was enjoying God's creation and was intently listening and looking for the Spirit's leadership in my life. My heavenly Father was communicating His love for me in a manner that gave me strength and confidence for life's journey. Here is my journal excerpt from my walk alone in the countryside on a sweltering summer day:

> What wonder and beauty, as I walked under a canopy of shade trees, buffered on either side with bushes and flowers. A narrow, slow moving creek made its way to my left, yes a hotbed for mosquitos and a haven for frogs, croaking for attention. Spiritually speaking this could have been my tunnel of darkness, with gnats buzzing and bugs berating me on every side. But His presence, like insect repellant, shielded me from fear and kept my self-reliance in check. Obstacles of faith are stepping stones in God's will.

> This is what the Lord says, "Stand at the crossroads and look; ask for the ancient paths, ask where the good way is, and walk in it, and you will find rest for your souls" (Jeremiah 6:16).

> After another 15 minutes, my shaded, cool canopy opened up into another crossroads between two additional cornfields and a barn. It felt like my childhood days in Alabama, with four tread worn, weed covered tractor tires stacked unstable on top of one another. This is where I read the sign, "Leave only your footprints and take only your pictures." I chuckled under my breath, because I could only leave footprints, since I left my phone back home with Rita for repair. I sucked down half of my water bottle as perspiration was making its way down my neck and back. Thirsty I was to taste God's goodness.

> I am big on metaphors and analogies. Some Wisdom Hunter devotional readers lovingly remind me how I sometimes get too excited trying to make thoughts, words, and sentences too memorable! Nevertheless, the cool water

on this hot midmorning reminded me that only the Holy Spirit can fill our thirsty souls. Careful not to take this analogy too far, I glanced down at the plastic water bottle and believe me, it said with bold branding, PURIFIED WATER!

Hallelujah the Spirit of God is pure in its elements and its application in our lives. I burst out into spontaneous praise and adoration of Almighty God. (It is easier to sing loud when only my Savior is listening.) At any moment He waits to quench our spiritual thirst! Yes, God's "Gatorade," so to speak, is refreshing and reenergizes us to stay in the game of life, for His glory. However, we must drink, before we dehydrate from noise and busyness!

"Let anyone who is thirsty come to me [Jesus] to drink. Whoever believes in me, as Scripture has said, rivers of living water will flow from within them" (John 7:37-38).

In the middle of my freedom in worship a fierce but gentle breeze stroked my beaded face of sweat, cooling my earthly body, whose spirit was indeed hot for heaven. Yes, the Holy Spirit was drawing me, I knew neither where this delightful wind came from nor where it was going, only that I must listen closely and follow boldly! What I experienced in the next few minutes is hard to explain, other than thoughts, "out of Christ's clear blue sky" began to flood my mind. Yes, over the years in my walk with Jesus, on "random" occasions, the Holy Spirit has seduced me by His love to listen intently to His passionate pleas, and this was one of those remarkable times of vision and intimacy! Be who I created you to be and I will take care of who you need to become.

"The wind blows wherever it pleases. You hear its sound, but you cannot tell where it comes from or where it is going. So it is with everyone born of the Spirit" (John 3:8).

TAKEAWAY: *Relational leaders have an attentive, listening heart, and an intent to obey.*

Relational Leaders Are Slow to Talk and Quick to Listen

"My dear brothers and sisters, take note of this: Everyone should be quick to listen, slow to speak and slow to become angry" (James 1:19). I have to work at being an active listener. At the end of a workday, my tendency is to talk too much about work with my wife, Rita. I am learning to inquire about her day first, before I bore her with too many of my work details. Passive listening is like listening to music in the background. Active listening is like listening to music with headphones on. My mental clutter disrupts my ability to concentrate on another's concerns. I pray for the discipline of organizing my thoughts so I am prepared to become an active listener. Active listeners focus on others.

James challenged his community of believers to talk less, listen more, and not harbor an angry attitude. Perhaps he had witnessed unhealthy interactions between those who should be treating each other with the utmost respect. James addressed his readers as brothers and sisters. This family of faith needed to raise the quality of their conversations. The better we get at knowing one another, the better we should be at anticipating one another's needs. "The more you talk, the more likely you will cross the line and say the wrong thing; but if you are wise, you'll speak less and with restraint" (Proverbs 10:19 The Voice). Passive listening easily misunderstands, but active listening gains insight. God blesses a heart that really wants to hear.

TAKEAWAY: *Relational leaders use active listening to gain insight.*

Heart-to-Heart Engagement

Who deserves your undivided attention? How can you show them that you really know them? If you want to engage in active listening, consider statements like, "You seem overwhelmed right now. I feel a lot of pressure as well, but I want us to support each other the best we can. How can I help you?" If someone expresses an uncommon complaint, repeat back to them the essence of their words. It shows you care. For example: "My body aches and my head really hurts." "It sounds like you don't feel well at all. You probably didn't sleep well, did you?" Active listening empathizes. Active listening is an essential habit for relational leaders.

> **Point to Ponder:** Active listening empathizes and engages the heart of another.

Listening Is One of the Best Ways to Extend Love to Another

How do we build our network of relationships? We lead the conversation with love and concern: "What are you most excited about in your life right now?" And we end the conversation with love: "What is the biggest challenge you are currently facing that I can pray about and with which I can help you?" Love looks to the interest of others. In the process, our interests either fade in significance or are creatively taken care of by Christ!

Allow the Lord to first love you by abiding in His presence. As a consequence, you will be willing and prepared to love others well at their point of need. In Christ, receive and extend love! We serve with success when we learn how best to listen to the Lord as we grow in our listening skills with others.

> **TAKEAWAY:** Relational leaders employ caring questions in order to grow their capacity to listen lovingly to others.

Summary of Chapter Twenty-Seven Takeaways

1. Relational leaders have an attentive, listening heart, and an intent to obey.

2. Relational leaders use active listening to gain insight.

3. Relational leaders employ caring questions in order to grow their capacity to listen lovingly to others.

Chapter Twenty-Eight

Engage in a Small, Caring Community

In Christ we, though many, form one body, and each member belongs to all the others.

ROMANS 12:5

The key to the happy life, it seems, is the good life: a life with sustained relationships, challenging work, and connections to community.

PAUL BLOOM

How Community Brings Restoration

Genesis 1 reminds us that human beings are made in the image of God. One key aspect of what it means to be human, therefore, is to live in community. God is a community of persons—Father, Son, and Holy Spirit—and so when we live in relational peace, unity, and self-giving love, we reflect this kind of community to the world around us.

I believe it is for this reason that isolation and the loss of community is so devastating. If you have ever had seasons of intentional friendship and meaningful community, people with whom you are truly doing life together, you know that it is an unspeakable gift. It brings a sense of belonging, purpose, and comfort. Likewise, if you find yourself alone, lonely, and isolated, you know the fear, pain, and heartache associated with that reality.

215

> **Point to Ponder:** *God is a community of persons—Father, Son, and Holy Spirit—and so when we live in relational peace, unity, and self-giving love, we reflect this kind of community to the world around us.*

In Mark's Gospel we find a story of Jesus healing a leper: "A leper came to him begging him, and kneeling he said to him, 'If you choose, you can make me clean.' Moved with pity, Jesus stretched out his hand and touched him, and said to him, 'I do choose. Be made clean!' Immediately the leprosy left him, and he was made clean" (Mark 1:40-42 NRSV). While the physical pain and discomfort from this skin condition was surely severe, I do not think it was the greatest need in this man's life. To be a leper in Jesus's day was to be ritually unclean, cast out from community and society, isolated from the very people you could call family and friends. When this man called out to Jesus, I believe the cry of his heart was a plea for belonging. "Lord, restore to me the gift of being known and knowing others!"

When Jesus looked at this leper, He had compassion for a beloved child who had lost an essential part of what it means to be human. In healing his leprosy, Jesus also restored to him the ability to reflect the nature of God by living life connected to others in meaningful and intimate ways. Take time to celebrate the gift of community in your life. Reach out to those who are close to you and let them know how grateful you are for them and their investment in your life. Likewise, if you find yourself identifying with the leper in this story, cling to hope and reach out to Jesus in your pain and loss, asking Him to look upon you with compassion and restore to you the gift of living life in community with others.

> **TAKEAWAY:** *Relational leaders engage in community in order to be known and to know others!*

Courage Incubates in Community

Courage needs community in order to thrive. The company of

other Christians instills boldness in my belief in Jesus. When I engage with other zealous lovers of the Lord, it energizes my faith. Whether standing together in corporate worship or gathered together in a conference around our common commitment to Christ—I am compelled to follow my calling. In a recent board meeting, each person shared a painful struggle and shared how we could pray for them. My heart swelled with uncommon courage to pray in faith. Courage is contagious.

> **Point to Ponder:** *The company of other Christians instills boldness in our beliefs.*

After the cross and resurrection, the disciples could have dispersed, but they stayed together. Why? These diverse Christ followers had newfound courage in their risen Lord and in their love for each other. "Afterward Jesus appeared again to his disciples, by the Sea of Galilee. It happened this way: Simon Peter, Thomas (also known as Didymus), Nathanael from Cana in Galilee, the sons of Zebedee, and two other disciples were together" (John 21:1-2). Peter the recovering denier, Thomas the former doubter, Nathanael the quiet but faithful follower—the ambitious sons of thunder (James and John), and two humble, behind the scenes, unnamed disciples—made up the core launch team for Christianity! What they lacked on their resumé they made up for in faith and courage. Together they were unstoppable! "When they saw the courage of Peter and John and realized that they were unschooled, ordinary men, they were astonished and they took note that these men had been with Jesus" (Acts 4:13).

Engaging with Other Christ Followers

How do you engage with other Christ followers? Worship, Bible study, prayer, suffering, service projects, Sunday school, community groups, board meetings, vacations, and mission trips are all good opportunities to give and receive courage. Christianity is not an individual sport. It is a team sport. Your giftedness, skills, and experience may feed your self-reliance—but you and others are better off when you are not aloof. Unselfish relational engagement protects you from a "me only" focus and frees you to boldly follow the Spirit's lead.

We all suffer in silence from time to time. Breaking our silence and seeking the support of others who understand and even experience the same struggles requires courage. Experts are another source of strength. Professionals can give us a third-party perspective that contributes to our comprehension and courage. Our confidence grows when we can grasp the "why" behind the "what" we are experiencing. Like the first disciples, we need to first see Jesus—then feel the loving support of friends. Courage comes from Christ and growing together with His followers! "Immediately he spoke to them and said, 'Take courage! It is I. Don't be afraid'" (Mark 6:50).

Heavenly Father, keep me close to Your children so I can courageously engage our culture with Your love.

TAKEAWAY: *Relational leaders seek the support of others who understand.*

A Community of Love

If someone on an elevator ride asked you to explain what it means that Christians believe in the Trinity, what would you say? If you were to respond by saying that God is one divine being existing eternally as three distinct yet equal persons, you would certainly be theologically correct, but you might leave them more confused than when they first asked! I've found one of the most helpful ways to speak of God as Trinity is to use the language of community. When we say that we believe in a triune God, fundamentally we are saying that we believe God is a community of love.

Have you ever heard it said that God created the world and human beings because He was lonely? I've heard this from time to time, but when we see God as a community of love, we must realize that there was never a time when God was alone! In fact, you could say that our very desire for community, to be known and know others, exists because we are made in the image of a communal God.

> **Point to Ponder:** *Our very desire for community, to be known and know others, exists because we are made in the image of a communal God.*

"Community" and "love" are two words that get thrown around a lot. We all seek community and want to be loved, so why is community so elusive and love so confusing? In part, I think it is because we are not exactly clear on what we are looking for! When we say that we value community, what do we actually mean? When we look for love, what are we looking for? As Christians, we learn how to live in community and how to love by looking to our triune God. We see the Father who in love sends the Son and Spirit (John 14:24-26), the Son who reveals the Father (Matthew 11:27), and the Spirit who glorifies the Son (John 16:14). It is here that we see three persons who exist for the good of the other. Here we see a love that gives itself so fully that it can't help but overflow and invite others into this way of being. Does your life reflect this kind of community? Is your family life at home characterized by this kind of radical, self-giving love?

Rather than thinking of the Trinity as an abstract Christian belief that is confusing or irrelevant, seek instead to see it as nothing less than the eternal community of love from which all love flows. The great mystery is that, as we are united to Christ, we are invited into this eternal community of love. As we respond to this invitation, we learn what it means to live in community, to love and be loved in return.

> **TAKEAWAY:** *Relational leaders learn how to live in community and how to love by looking to the triune God.*

Summary of Chapter Twenty-Eight Takeaways

1. Relational leaders engage in community in order to be known and to know others!

2. Relational leaders seek the support of others who understand.

3. Relational leaders learn how to live in community and how to love by looking to the triune God.

Chapter Twenty-Nine

Mentor and Be Mentored

*For this reason I have sent to you Timothy, my son whom
I love, who is faithful in the Lord. He will remind
you of my way of life in Christ Jesus, which agrees
with what I teach everywhere in every church.*

1 Corinthians 4:17

*The mediocre mentor tells.
The good mentor explains.
The superior mentor demonstrates.
The greatest mentors inspire!*

Lucia Ballas Traynor

A Heart for Mentoring

A heart for mentoring is motivated by love: love for God and love for people to grow in grace and love for God. I have been blessed by multiple mentors over the years. Men loved me where I was, but they loved me too much to allow me to remain where I was in my relationship with Christ, my wife, children, family, or friends. Because these men intentionally invested in me—I seek to prayerfully invest time, energy, and money in other men. I am an imperfect person helping other imperfect people grow in the perfect love of Jesus.

Paul affectionally refers to Timothy as his son in the faith. "You then, my son, be strong in the grace that is in Christ Jesus. And the things you have heard me say in the presence of many witnesses entrust to reliable people who will also be qualified to teach others. Join with me in suffering, like a good soldier of Christ Jesus" (2 Timothy 2:1-3). The older Paul saw potential in the younger Timothy. Timothy's humility made him teachable and a worthy candidate to grow stronger in the grace of Christ Jesus. Paul boldly challenged Timothy in the presence of others to select qualified men who would also teach other men. Like training a good soldier, effective mentoring requires discipline, sacrifice, and suffering.

Mentors engage with those who want a better life. Invest in reliable people who will invest in other reliable people. "Teach them his decrees and instructions, and show them the way they are to live and how they are to behave. Select capable men from all the people—men who fear God, trustworthy men who hate dishonest gain—and appoint them as officials" (Exodus 18:20-21). If you wait to mentor until you feel perfectly qualified, you will never mentor. Those who influence the most feel the least qualified. They are vulnerable with their own struggles, sins, and shortcomings. Mentees can relate to mentors who are honest about their insecurities, fears, and failures. Like Paul, invite sincere seekers to join you in your journey with Jesus through life. The great adventure of faith is not without tests and trials. But together—young and old, mentee and mentor—we can persevere. Start with one who wants to grow—then expand into a small community.

> **Point to Ponder:** If you wait to mentor until you feel perfectly qualified, you will never mentor.

You might say, "Where do I start?" Begin in prayer. Ask the Lord to lead you to people who have a passion to grow in their faith, character, and relationships. "Let the morning bring me word of your unfailing love, for I have put my trust in you. Show me the way I should go for to you I entrust my life" (Psalm 143:8). Most of all, lean into the Holy Spirit to teach your mind and heart. Mentors are loved by God.

Heavenly Father, lead me to love and mentor
others in a way that grows them in Your love.

> **TAKEAWAY:** Relational leaders are imperfect people who help other imperfect people grow in the perfect love of God.

The Gift of Mentorship

My friend Woody, along with many others, was mentored by Truett Cathy (Chick-fil-A Founder and CEO). Even as he approached his pending death, Truett reminded Woody what was most important in life, "Love your wife well and take care of your children." With one foot in heaven and one foot on earth, Truett used his influence for the benefit of one man. A few days later at Truett's funeral, Woody honored his mentor with these words (reflecting on a time Truett and Woody delivered lemon pie to a widow):

> Truett, you took to heart the scripture found in James 1:26: "Religion that God our Father accepts as pure and faultless is this; to look after orphans and widows in their distress and to keep oneself from being polluted by the world." Here you were showing Christ's love to a widow while modeling a servant's heart for this orphan. That's why, decades later, I found myself—along with some little Faulk girls—delivering homemade Dwarf House pies and Chick-fil-A food to homes and the homeless on Christmas Eve. It wasn't until I dropped a pie off at the home of a widower I cared about that it dawned on me— you had modeled behavior that I was now doing. You, Truett, taught me how to be generous. I had become... just like you.

In a similar way, as Paul approached the end of his life, he reminded the leaders of the church what was most important for them. "Now I commit you to God and to the word of his grace, which can build you up...remembering the words the Lord Jesus himself said: 'It is more blessed to give than to receive.' When Paul had finished speaking, he knelt down with all of them and prayed. They all wept as they embraced him and kissed him" (Acts 20:32, 35-37).

He committed them to God, knowing the Lord was their ultimate leader. Paul's influence marked their lives, but Christ was their master. Paul also committed them to God's word of grace which would build them up in faith, love, and generosity, reminding them of Jesus's words of additional blessings that come to generous givers. Then, in humility, all knelt in prayer, weeping and crying together, experiencing their last time together.

> **Point to Ponder:** *A mentor leaves her mark on a person's life, but Christ is the master over that person's life.*

A Mentor to Mentors

You may not feel like a mentor to mentors, but the Lord will grow your faith and influence to a season of life to serve in this way. When you are a mentor to mentors, it's not about you, but about those who are patiently, gently, and prayerfully served by you. Pray about one person you can pour into with life lessons you have learned by walking with Christ over the years. Be real about your many mistakes, failures, and struggles. Honesty and vulnerability connect hearts to each other and to Jesus. When you take the time to prayerfully mentor potential mentors, you invite the Spirit's power on earth and give cause for praise in heaven.

Children in the faith who are nurtured in their love for Christ become God's instrument of peace, love, and hope for their generation. Do not despise whatever role you have in life: parent, retiree, community volunteer, teacher, administrator, or service professional. Pray that God would use you to grow others in God's Word and grace. The human heart and mind are hungry for love and truth. Share love and truth with humility and compassion and watch the Holy Spirit work in you and in those whom you love unconditionally. Mentor and be mentored so the Kingdom of Light illuminates brighter than the Kingdom of Darkness. A mentor for Jesus is a mighty weapon in the hands of God. Bow in humble prayer—He will lift you up!

Heavenly Father, give me courage to mentor
others for You. In Jesus's name, amen.

TAKEAWAY: *Relational leaders mentor with humility and compassion and watch the Holy Spirit work in those they love unconditionally.*

Mentor the Emerging Generation

Most young people yearn for someone to invest time and wisdom in them. They know deep in their hearts they need help handling their heartaches. They need wise and loving instruction. Who in your circle of influence is a candidate for your caring attention? It may be a son or daughter, a colleague at work, or a friend from church. God places people in our lives for a purpose. Prayerfully pursue a mentor relationship with a teachable young person. They can learn from your mistakes as much or more as from your wise choices. Mentors are not perfect, just wiser because of failures and successes. Look around and ask the Lord to lead you to a young person who may be edging toward the wrong direction. Reach out and you will have returned the favor to someone who loved you.

Point to Ponder: Prayerfully pursue a mentoring relationship with a teachable young person.

Mentors take time for others because they are eternally grateful for those who took time for them. Gratitude to God is a great reason to go the extra mile with someone younger. Read books together; maybe a book a month for a year. Meet over coffee to discuss how the book challenged your thinking or changed your behavior for the better.

A young leader can avoid certain problems when she is able to model the wise habits of her mentor. Always invite an older adult into your life who can educate you in the ways of God. Be like Timothy, who welcomed Paul's instruction: "Timothy, my son, I am giving you this command in keeping with the prophecies once made about you, so that by recalling them you may fight the battle well" (1 Timothy 1:18). The mentoring process is valuable to both parties. Mentoring provides accountability, encouragement, love, and obedience to Christ's commands. Mentor young people so they follow the right path, and in turn, help someone else do the same.

TAKEAWAY: *Relational leaders invest time, wisdom, and resources in others.*

> The best way a mentor can prepare another leader is to expose him or her to other great people.
>
> John C. Maxwell

Summary of Chapter Twenty-Nine Takeaways

1. Relational leaders are imperfect people who help other imperfect people grow in the perfect love of God.

2. Relational leaders mentor with humility and compassion and watch the Holy Spirit work in those they love unconditionally.

3. Relational leaders invest time, wisdom, and resources in others.

Chapter Thirty

Grow a Loving Relationship with God

We love because he first loved us.

1 JOHN 4:19

Love for God is obedience; love for God is holiness. To love God and to love man is to be conformed to the image of Christ, and this is salvation.

CHARLES SPURGEON

A Fresh Infusion of God's Love Empowers Us to Love Others Well

Jesus gave His disciples a command: "A new command I give you: Love one another. As I have loved you, so you must love one another. By this everyone will know that you are my disciples, if you love one another" (John 13:34-35). Of course, not everyone is easy to love! Many people live defeated by their shame. Consumed with their hurt, some people easily hurt others and are closed to comfort and care, at least initially. They nurse their pain, they refuse to receive counsel, and they remain stuck in self-pity. We have all been there—we're mad at ourselves for unidentifiable reasons, we scowl and our posture betrays our lack of morale; we're unable to deliver ourselves and unwilling to ask for help. Only patient, kind, and gentle love administered in persistent doses can penetrate some hearts. Love never fails!

God's love is far superior to man's love. The Lord's love is perfect; man's is imperfect. Christ's love is unconditional; man's love is conditional. The love of God is limitless; the love of man is limited. Divine love is diverse; human love is like-minded. Our heavenly Father's love far exceeds even an earthly father whose love is admirable. Our Lord lavishes His love on us so that we can lavishly love others.

> **Point to Ponder:** Our Lord lavishes His love on us so we can lavishly love others.

We are loved by the Lord to love for the Lord. Indeed, we are called by Christ to love with a love that is not of this world. It is a love that can only be explained by an encounter with Almighty God. God's transforming power inspires His disciples to love as His representatives. In His parting words, our Savior introduced how His disciples were to love. "We know and rely on the love God has for us. God is love. Whoever lives in love lives in God, and God in them" (1 John 4:16). His command and promises, faithfully followed by His disciples, are the best apologetic for faith.

Our responsibility to love and serve starts with our brothers and sisters in the faith. If we ignore those in need or "shoot our wounded," we become unattractive to an unloved world. Those who already live according to a low moral standard have little interest in exchanging it for another low moral standard. However, when we live out the Lord's unconditional love for one another, we become attractive to the unsaved. A fellow believer caught in sin needs our loving restoration, not our harsh condemnation. As Thomas Merton said, "The beginning of love is to let those we love be perfectly themselves, and not to twist them to fit our own image. Otherwise we love only the reflection of ourselves we find in them."[6]

Our love for the Lord is evident when we do what we know to be true. Our obedience to our loving heavenly Father draws other potential disciples into our Father's forgiving arms of grace. I show my love for another child of God when I honor God. Like siblings whose love for each other grows as they honor their parents, so Christians who honor their heavenly Father grow in their love for one another. We become Christ's channel to love like Him. "Dear friends, since God so loved us, we also ought to love one another. No one has ever seen God;

but if we love one another, God lives in us and his love is made complete in us" (1 John 4:11-12).

> **TAKEAWAY:** *Relational leaders receive God's love in their life so they have the capacity to love others in need of unconditional love.*

Relational Leaders Provide Loving Hospitality to Others

Love is irresistible for those in search of a Savior. Everyone whose heart aches for authentic relationship will take notice when they see Christians love one another. Parents who encourage and build up their sons and daughters are a magnet to their children's friends who live lonely lives in discouraging and disruptive home environments.

Have you thought of your home as a sanctuary for seeking souls? Every time a neighbor drops by, a friend stays overnight, or you host a party for your child's team, you have an opportunity to model the love of Jesus toward those you know and to those whom you meet for the first time. "Share with the Lord's people who are in need. Practice hospitality" (Romans 12:13). Leverage love for the Lord, and He will draw people to Himself.

Being a disciple of Jesus does have its benefits, and being loved is close to the top. When you placed your faith in Christ, you became a giver and receiver of Christian love. Do not resist the righteous care that Christ followers extend to you. Be glad you model the love of God's children that can melt the hearts of outside observers. "Why," they ask, "do people give so much, expecting nothing in return?"

How do you intentionally love your brothers and sisters in Christ? Paul urged the Galatian churches to "serve one another humbly in love" (Galatians 5:13). How do you serve humbly in love? Do you share relationships, money, your vacation home, your primary residence, or your car? It may be showing up during a health issue, praying for a job interview, babysitting their little one, or mowing their grass. Unbelievers take notice when believers lavishly love each other.

The Lord seeks not only to love us, but to love through us. His love removes our insensitive heart and replaces it with sensitivity to His Spirit. The Almighty's agape love rearranges our priorities around the needs of others first. His love teaches us to first comfort people in their pain and then wait for the appropriate time to administer truth. This kind of unconditional love is a conduit for the lost to know Christ.

Point to Ponder: *Love is irresistible for those in search of a Savior.*

TAKEAWAY: *Relational leaders love others through hospitality.*

A Loving Relationship with God Praises Him

Jesus was full of the Holy Spirit and full of joy over God's revelation of truth. His joy exploded in thanksgiving to His heavenly Father. Knowledge of the Holy One is hidden from the intellectually proud, but is revealed to the humble in heart. "At that time Jesus, full of joy through the Holy Spirit, said, 'I praise you, Father, Lord of heaven and earth, because you have hidden these things from the wise and learned, and revealed them to little children. Yes, Father, for this is what you were pleased to do'" (Luke 10:21). Self-proclaimed sages could not see what babies in the faith came to understand: Jesus Christ was the Son of God. Prophets and kings longed to see and hear from the Messiah, but the meek disciples were the first to experience their Savior Jesus. It is an extraordinary gift to see with eternal eyes what the Lord has in store for those who love Him.

It is astounding to consider that, through the Holy Spirit, we can know God. Our heavenly Father is available to show us Himself and to reveal to us His will and His ways. We can receive through a humble and contrite heart what conceited scholars miss. Our Lord chose us to champion His truth because our human credentials are very modest compared to the surpassing glory of our Savior Jesus Christ. The Holy Spirit reveals to us what we need to know for today's decisions.

As a sovereign king has control over a country, the Spirit is sovereign over truth's revelation.

> **Point to Ponder:** *We deflect people's praise as a sacrifice of worship to the Lord God Almighty.*

Joy wells up in our hearts and explodes into thanksgiving when we recall the revelation of God. His Spirit convicts us of our need to repent of our sin and receive Christ and His love as the payment for our sin. We rejoice knowing that our name is written in heaven. It is an extraordinary blessing to have the assurance of eternal life with the Lord and with all those who love Him. Indeed, we thank our Father for the privilege and opportunity to learn how to walk with Jesus and invite others to know Him. We are Christ's channel to reveal grace and truth to needy souls.

How can you express gratitude to God for the forgiveness of your sins? What are some evidences of the joy of the Lord in your life? Praise and thanksgiving to the Almighty are fruits of a joyful heart. "Sing joyfully to the LORD, you righteous; it is fitting for the upright to praise him" (Psalm 33:1). Thank Him when you see the smile on the face of a loved one who has experienced a stroke. Though unable to speak, they can hum hymns and tear up at the reading of God's Word. The revelation of Jesus Christ is extraordinary to those with an eye on their eternal dwelling! As Paul says, "For we know that if the earthly tent we live in is destroyed, we have a building from God, an eternal house in heaven, not built by human hands" (2 Corinthians 5:1).

> **TAKEAWAY:** *Relational leaders who walk in the fullness of the Holy Spirit exude joy that attracts others to Jesus.*

A Prayer for Loving Like Jesus

Dear Jesus—lover of my soul,

When I bow in humility, You lift me up by Your generous love,

*When I sing joyful praises, You fill my heart to
overflowing with Your abundant love,*

*When I weep tears of sorrow, You soothe
my soul with Your comforting love,*

*When I timidly share my doubts, You boldly
infuse my faith with Your confident love,*

*When I am unsure of what to do, You pour out
Your loving wisdom to show me the way,*

*When fear floods my feelings, You flush
me clean with Your perfect love,*

*When conflict crushes my spirit, You meld the
pieces together with Your healing love,*

When I am weary, You provide rest with Your peaceful love,

*Lover of my soul, I lean into Your lavish love
so I might love others for You and to You.*

*Thank You precious Jesus for embracing me for who I am,
and for releasing me to be a radical lover of You and others,*

amen.

God loved us first, so we could love others.

1 John 4:19

Summary of Chapter Thirty Takeaways

1. Relational leaders receive God's love in their life so they have the capacity to love others in need of unconditional love.

2. Relational leaders love others through hospitality.

3. Relational leaders who walk in the fullness of the Holy Spirit exude joy that attracts others to Jesus.

Conclusion:
Stay Fresh in Your
Walk with Jesus

Relational leadership is built on a growing relationship with Jesus Christ. There are no shortcuts and no formulas—just faith and love in the One who is perfect love. When we surrender our will to God's will, God renews our mind with the mind of Christ and guards our heart under the Spirit's affections, we are positioned to be a relational leader who glorifies the Lord. Henri Nouwen states it well:

> Leadership must be rooted in the permanent, intimate relationship with the incarnate Word, Jesus, and they need to find there the source for their words, advice, and guidance...Dealing with burning issues without being rooted in a deep personal relationship with God easily leads to divisiveness because, before we know it, our sense of self is caught up in our opinion about a given subject. But when we are securely rooted in personal intimacy with the source of life, it will be possible to remain flexible without being relativistic, convinced without being rigid, willing to confront without being offensive, gentle and forgiving without being soft, and true witness without being manipulative.[7]

As we mature in the faith, the more we recognize our weaknesses, the more we can become stronger because of the work of God's grace in our inner being. Relational leaders who are tethered to trust in Christ have an inner stability and peace that affects our work and home culture. Stay fresh in your walk with Jesus, and you will infuse your environment with energy and encouragement. Relationships matter when your relationship with the Lord matters the most.

I will leave you with the apostle Paul's prayer in Ephesians 3:14-21:

> For this reason I kneel before the Father, from whom every family in heaven and on earth derives its name. I pray that out of his glorious riches he may strengthen you with power through His Spirit in your inner being, so that Christ may dwell in your hearts through faith. And I pray that you, being rooted and established in love, may have power, together with all the Lord's holy people, to grasp how wide and long and high and deep is the love of Christ, and to know this love that surpasses knowledge—that you may be filled to the measure of all the fullness of God. Now to him who is able to do immeasurably more than all we ask or imagine, according to his power that is at work within us, to him be glory in the church and in Christ Jesus throughout all generations, for ever and ever! Amen.

Notes

1. Henri Nouwen, *In the Name of Jesus* (New York: Crossroad, 1992), 61.

2. Henri Nouwen, *Compassion* (New York: Image Books, 1983), 107.

3. https://www.huffingtonpost.com/cindy-jonesnyland/how-gratitude-leads-to-ge_b_8690052.html.

4. Taken from https://www.all4kids.org/2016/05/03/creating-safe-open-home-environment/. Used with permission of Children's Bureau of Southern California.

5. *Christian Post* at https://www.christianpost.com/news/second-mile-service.html.

6. Thomas Merton, *No Man Is an Island* (New York: Harvest Books, 2002).

7. Henri Nouwen, *In the Name of Jesus: Reflections on Christian Leadership* (New York: Crossroad, 1992), page 45.

About Boyd and Rita Bailey

Rita graduated from Gadsden State Jr. College with a Medical Lab Tech associates degree in 1980. Boyd graduated from Snead State Jr. College, Jacksonville State University, and then Southwestern Baptist Theological Seminary in 1985. They worked in churches for ten years, including Boyd as associate pastor at First Baptist Atlanta with Dr. Charles Stanley and his son, Andy. The Stanleys gave Boyd the opportunity to write for some of their published books and taught Boyd and Rita lifelong lessons about servant leadership, loving people, prayer, and teaching the Bible.

In 1995, Boyd and Rita opened the Crown Ministries office in Atlanta and helped churches disciple their members in wise financial principles. The ministry grew significantly and Boyd was eventually asked to serve as the national field director over 32 offices across the country. Soon after 9/11, with four teenage daughters at home, Boyd and Rita cofounded Ministry Ventures, where they trained and coached ministry leaders in the best practices of prayer, board development, strategy, administration, and fundraising. For 14 years they helped more than 1,000 ministries become their best.

Wisdom Hunters is another ministry God birthed in 2004 to help people "apply unchanging truth in a changing world" though sound biblical teaching and application. Over 250,000 daily readers in 86 countries are reached through email, social media, an app, a blog, audio, a podcast, and YouVersion. By God's grace, ten books have been self-published and eight books published with Harvest House, including *Learning to Lead Like Jesus*. Boyd likes to say, "I am not a great writer, but I am able to write about great things!"

Boyd and Rita serve on numerous boards, including Ministry Ventures, Wisdom Hunters, Souly Business, and The River Foundation. Rita serves on the Hello Hope board and is deeply involved in Spiritual Formations. They both love traveling, hiking, and loving on the grandbabies. Since 2016, Boyd has served as the president of National Christian Foundation of Georgia, helping 1,100 families manage donor-advised funds with over $40M given annually to Christian causes.

They have four daughters, four sons-in-law, and nine grandbabies. Boyd and Rita are most grateful to Jesus Christ for His love, forgiveness, and intimate relationship that gives them the courage, energy, and love to wake up every day to serve and love people. Fun fact: Rita recently served in the Amazon jungle, loving on children through medicine and vacation Bible school, while Boyd sailed in the British Virgin Islands!

WISDOM HUNTERS

H e who walks with wise men will be wise, but the companion of fools will suffer harm" (Proverbs 13:20 NASB).

In 2003, Boyd Bailey began to informally email personal reflections from his morning devotional time to a select group of fellow wisdom hunters. Over time, these informal emails grew into Wisdom Hunters Daily Devotional. Today, thanks to God's favor and faithful followers, these emails and social media posts reach more than 150,000 readers each day.

Boyd remains relentless in the pursuit of wisdom and continues to daily write raw, original, real-time reflections from his personal encounters with the Lord.

Visit www.WisdomHunters.com where you can:

- Subscribe to free daily devotional emails
- Find out how to access our blog, Facebook, Twitter, Instagram, and the new Wisdom Hunters podcast
- Choose from a wide selection of devotional books on marriage, wisdom, wise living, and money; with books also for graduates, fathers, mothers, and more (eBook and print versions available)
- Download the free Wisdom Hunters app for Apple and Android

The thoughtful comments and wisdom our followers share each day can help us all in our journey with God.

Founded in 1982 and based in Atlanta, Georgia, the National Christian Foundation (NCF) is a charitable giving ministry that provides wise giving solutions, mobilizes resources, and inspires biblical generosity for Christian families, advisors, and charities. NCF is currently the ninth-largest US nonprofit, having accepted more than $9 billion in contributions. It has granted more than $7 billion to more than 40,000 charities. The NCF Giving Fund, or donor-advised fund, allows donors to make charitable contributions and then recommend grants to the charities they care about, over time. NCF is also an industry leader in accepting gifts of appreciated assets, such as stocks, real estate, and business interests, which enables donors to save on taxes and align their charitable goals with their family, business, estate, and legacy plans. Learn more about NCF at www.NCFgiving.com.

Other Leadership Reading
by Boyd Bailey

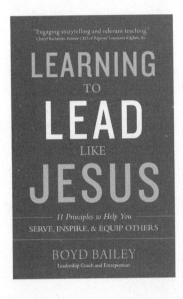

Learning to Lead Like Jesus

It's incredible when someone uses their gifts to make you feel valued and inspire you to greatness. What does it take to develop that kind of heart and influence? How can you become a leader like Jesus?

Join Boyd Bailey as he shows you how to mirror Jesus's heart and make a positive difference in those around you. Explore 11 common traits that mark successful leaders, and learn the keys to growth in wisdom and humility. Through practical teaching, you will find that great leadership begins when you turn your focus to God and model Him in your attitude, conversations, and actions.

A faithful life and humble spirit make you a leader worth following. When you lean into the Lord and learn from His example of perfect leadership, you will see lives transformed—beginning with your own!

More Great Harvest House
Books by Boyd Bailey

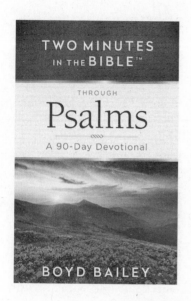

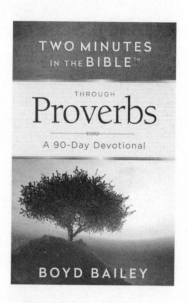

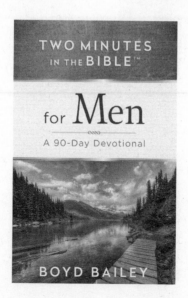

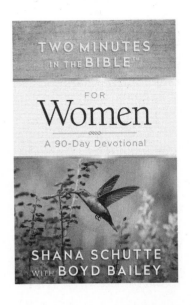

TWO MINUTES IN THE BIBLE™
FOR
Women
A 90-Day Devotional

SHANA SCHUTTE
WITH BOYD BAILEY

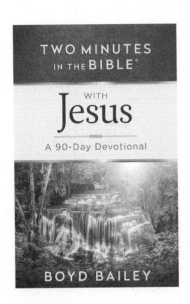

TWO MINUTES IN THE BIBLE®
WITH
Jesus
A 90-Day Devotional

BOYD BAILEY

TWO MINUTES IN THE BIBLE®
THROUGH
Revelation
A 90-Day Devotional

BOYD BAILEY

To learn more about Harvest House books and
to read sample chapters, visit our website:

www.harvesthousepublishers.com